# Creating New Markets in the Digital Economy

*Creating New Markets in the Digital Economy: Value and Worth* looks at how digitisation is radically changing the way we buy and experience products and services. Sharing her unique perspective of both business and academia, Irene Ng examines the implications of digital connectivity, including the need to design and scale future business models to better fit 'lived lives', creating value as well as increasing worth so that new markets can emerge. The book provides a conceptual framework and practical advice to equip readers with the knowledge they need to develop future products and services that take advantage of connectivity and serve contexts better. With its accessible language, numerous case examples and illustrations to illuminate challenging concepts, this book is an important resource for business leaders, entrepreneurs and policy-makers, as well as students of service science, business and engineering.

IRENE C. L. NG is Professor of Marketing and Service Systems and Director of the International Institute of Product and Service Innovation (IIPSI) at WMG, University of Warwick, UK. She was an entrepreneur for sixteen years as CEO of SA Tours, one of the largest tour operators in Southeast Asia, and the founder of Empress Cruise Lines, which she built into a venture worth US$250 million in annual turnover when she sold it in 1996. Since becoming an academic in 1997, Professor Ng has received global recognition for her work in value, new business models and service systems, with twenty-two journal articles, three books and national appointments such as the ESRC/AIM Services Fellow in 2008 and ESRC/NIHR Fellow in 2009.

# Creating New Markets in the Digital Economy

## Value and Worth

IRENE C.L. NG

Cover image and cartoons created by Elizabeth Shi-Yin Ho

CAMBRIDGE
UNIVERSITY PRESS

# CAMBRIDGE
## UNIVERSITY PRESS

University Printing House, Cambridge CB2 8BS, United Kingdom

Published in the United States of America by Cambridge University Press, New York

Cambridge University Press is part of the University of Cambridge.

It furthers the University's mission by disseminating knowledge in the pursuit of education, learning and research at the highest international levels of excellence.

www.cambridge.org
Information on this title: www.cambridge.org/9781107627420

First published 2014

Printed and bound in the United Kingdom by CPI Group Ltd, Croydon CR0 4YY

*A catalogue record for this publication is available from the British Library*

*Library of Congress Cataloguing in Publication data*
Ng, Irene C. L.
   Creating new markets in the digital economy : value and worth /
Irene C.L. Ng.
      pages cm
Includes bibliographical references and index.
ISBN 978-1-107-04935-2 (Hardback) – ISBN 978-1-107-62742-0 (Paperback)
1. Information technology–Economic aspects.   2. Technological innovations–
Economic aspects.   3. New products.   4. Value.   5. Market research.   I. Title.
HC79.I55N52 2014
658.8'72–dc23   2013028612

ISBN 978-1-107-04935-2 Hardback
ISBN 978-1-107-62742-0 Paperback

*For my Father*

# Contents

# Figures

# Table

# Preface

This book articulates a thinking journey, one that I embarked on since beginning my academic vocation in 1997, to get to the bottom of the economic notion of 'utility'. At that time, I was driven to understand how, when and why people purchase and how firms could price better; these became the subject of my first book, *The Pricing and Revenue Management of Services*.

This journey has since evolved into a quest to understand the fundamentals of value and the markets created from it. On this journey, I spent some time with sociology where I considered the human agency, identity and practices to create value; systems thinking, for a holistic view of value creation; business models, in terms of capturing, proposing and creating value; and information and communications technology (ICT), which I felt would inform future contexts for value creation. I also spent time with engineering, researching into the design of offerings that could potentially create value, and this became the subject of my second collaborative and edited book, *Complex Engineering Service Systems: Concepts and Research*.

While I don't believe the journey is complete yet, it has helped me develop a deeper understanding of how these different destinations come together to inform a very different future. It has also helped me reach certain conclusions about my own discipline of marketing, which I present as a postscript to the book.

I have also decided to write this book as a personal account, documenting much of what I have been thinking about from observing human behaviour, doing research and working with companies big and small over the past fifteen years. The theories I have drawn on are the foundations upon which many of my ideas

and thoughts have been made possible. Wherever I can, I have
created footnotes so that those interested in delving deeper may
read further. I have, however, chosen a style of writing that enables
me to inform the non-academic, the advanced practitioner and the
entrepreneur. This means that I may need to explain some basics,
but where I do so, it is to build upon that understanding to
communicate further thinking. By creating a progressive synthesis
of research with practice, I can also serve future researchers in this
domain.

One of the motivations for writing this book is the advent
of the 'Internet of Things' (IoT). I have increasingly felt the need
for work in this space to be grounded on more than just data sets
resulting from connected devices and sensors, just because it is
possible. I have no quarrel at all with big data and analytics,
but I do feel the need to theorise better so as to inform the
continued advancement of IoT applications and new markets arising
from them.

Theorising exposes the 'why' question (i.e., why should we have
connected things?), and facing up to that question holds the key to
how digital connectivity can improve the quality of our lives. In
theorising, I choose to take an approach that begins with the
individual, and by doing so, I hope to promote a digital technology
focus that begins with how we live our lives, rather than starting with
challenges of machine-to-machine communications. There is a
tendency when we focus on smart or connected firms, technologies,
cities and/or communities, to forget the person.

Digital connectivity now allows for greater voice, empowerment
and action of the person individually, and for them to get into groups
for collective, powerful and yet diverse voices. It allows us to
personalise everything for ourselves deeply and to live unique
individual lives even while many of these technologies are fully
scalable to offer into the market. The notion of firms creating viability
from serving only a subset of their customers (the segmentation issue)
and having to trade off product attributes, is increasingly becoming

archaic. The new way of thinking is how to allow for deep personalisation for all individuals while benefiting from increasing returns to scale.

Considering how this might be possible is the focus of this book. It will not come from existing mindsets. It will come from liberating the mind and considering how the good use of digital connectivity, overhauling the business model and redesigning a hybrid product and service offering could empower, rather than passively serve, customers. In a rapidly advancing world of digital technology, staying with the status quo is not an option. Disruption is never far off and no firm is too big to fail.

With an empowered and actionable voice, we are beginning to reinvent our roles both as customers and as employees. This creates tensions for those who have managed and controlled from some centralised location as they see more heterogeneity, variety and complexity in their 'system', be it the market, the firm or the business. Their perception is that the system is becoming more fractious, and this threatens its stability and in turn, their ability to manage and control. They are not wrong. What they do need to understand though is that empowered individuals will not be going away. This book hopes to bring some systematic insights into how we could see them as opportunities, and to tap into personalisation by individuals as customers of new markets.

The research is continuing and I am ever grateful for those who have contributed to my team's passion in service systems and value research. The book itself may still be too academic and abstract for some, while others may see immediate connections. My editors and I have discussed this several times and I don't think we can ever get it right. Telling it in this more abstracted way is necessary because I would like to ensure that whether you are looking at it from different sectors, firms, products or services, the lessons learnt are the same and to do that, this book must inevitably be more theoretical. Yet, I have endeavoured to use examples and anecdotes to illustrate these abstract concepts as best I can, so that they can be made more concrete. I must also say that this a 'how to think about' rather than a 'how to do' book. I will leave it to the many consultants out there to operationalise this into concrete action to assist firms.

We live in an age where a few centuries of research have yielded many insights, but these are not often put together in meaningful ways. Particularly in business, we have relied on the collaboration of academics, consultants and practitioners to translate good academic research into action by first translating the research into teaching materials, and then imparting them within the classroom. Yet, as our knowledge evolves, I have found that we are increasingly teaching disciplinary components but not their connections, with the belief that connections sit in practice.

This lack of academic synthesis to inform both the distinctiveness and connectiveness of disciplines is a great shame because the potential for knowledge is already there, but it seems inaccessible or is seen to be irrelevant as each discipline creates its own jargon. Synthesis is therefore a form of representation that allows us to move forward in our learning. There is theory in synthesis because the mere act of synthesising disciplinary knowledge uncovers both the consistencies and contradictions.

The objective of the book is simple. If you read it and learn something that will enable you to go on to innovate and give the world something special, I have achieved my purpose. As the director of a technology-focused innovation institute, I am passionate about helping technologists learn about value and markets, and I am always happy when they create pathways to commercialise their inventions. I have great faith in human creativity and inventiveness, especially when applied to engineering and digital technology. I find equal joy in doing the research, writing papers and books as well as in mentoring start-ups and bringing them to market.

Humanity is facing many great challenges – looking after our ageing population, keeping our children safe, providing clean water to so many who have none, improving our health, leading more fulfilling lives and creating more sustainable approaches to growth.

We need better technologies that work well with lives. My only lament is that while there are many programmes out there to help entrepreneurs succeed, there are very few that try to help technologists think about how their particular bit of 'thing' that they have made could create markets and change the world, or not. My approach aims to help those who are looking for some of these answers.

By doing so, I hope to address what Stephen Markham and his co-authors call the 'valley of death' between incubating a technology start-up and achieving scalable revenues. I do so by building a metaphorical bridge across that valley, which I believe comes about from understanding a particular technology's role in creating value and worth from the perspective of those who would buy and use them within their value-creating systems. Armed with this knowledge, technologists can construct their business models to be more successful in bringing their innovations to market. Currently, we rely very much on the goodwill of existing entrepreneurs, many of whom are brilliant and have done much good but whose knowledge, unfortunately, is not well codified.

Business researchers have always struggled with how to advise about the future when the only information which can be obtained is on the past and the present. My personal solution is through theorising. They say hindsight is always 20/20 , so a rear-view mirror can help us drive forward only when we theorise about what world could be in front of us. Theorising is a difficult skill but one which we must promote and preserve. Theorising is to piece together the logic created from the research and practice of the past, and propose what might be possible in the future. In a world of radical and disruptive technologies, data alone is unable to predict a future. Good theorising not only can predict possible futures, but can help us invent them. It helps us create the art of what's possible. Theorising helps children with imagined possibilities, just as it helps firms with new and radical innovations.

The world needs its theorists just as much as we need our empiricists. We must commend Einstein for theorising on relativity as much as we admire Eddington for proving it. We should be intrigued by Higgs theorising that a particle now called Higgs-Boson could exist, and applaud the particle physicists that search for it. In business as well, we need our theorists to propose what could be possible and our empiricists to prove or dispel them. This book therefore takes on the research that has been conducted and theorises on how we can think of new things, new business models and new markets of the future. By theorising, thinking and tinkering with what we know now and logically synthesising relevant research and practice, I hope to describe not only why and how new offerings come about, but how we can think of inventing them and paying for them so that even better offerings could be produced.

In writing this book, I have also been informed by my own use of digital technologies. Many who know me will know I am inseparable from my devices. I interact socially on Facebook, LinkedIn, Google+ and Twitter, and I often blog. I communicate on Facebook messenger, Skype, WhatsApp, Viber, email and text. My entire wardrobe is on an app on my iPad that enables me to choose what I wish to wear, matching colours and looks, without getting out of bed. It allows me to have a wardrobe that, if physically displayed, would be impossible unless I had a million-dollar mansion with a walk-in wardrobe the size of my current house. As a fan of Bordeaux reds, my wines stored both with my agent and at home are also categorised and accessible through an app. This is the same with money, stocks and shares. My running routes, pace and timings are collected through the RunKeeper app. Although not a good runner, I like being supported by my friends and the app allows my Facebook and Twitter friends to follow my runs (I appear as a little dot on their screen). Through the app, I can also take on live 'cheers' from friends when I participate in live events such as 5 km and 10 km races and half-marathons.

My life involves trying to manage a family and a research team, leading an innovation institute and travelling around the world. Technology plays a big part in allowing me to do all this, and yet feel serene enough at every location to write a book. More than two-thirds of this book was written on my iPad on planes, airports, beaches, shopping malls, cafes and in bed. When I am done, every change is uploaded onto the cloud where my editors and assistants can pick up the manuscript and work on it wherever they are and whenever they wish. Sketches were 'pencilled' by me using the Penultimate app and automatically uploaded onto Dropbox where the graphic artist can see them as her job list to create the comic art.

Of course, my family complains about my 'unholy' attachment to my devices; one Christmas, they created an 'Irene's iPad' persona on Facebook which proceeded to become 'friends' with all my Facebook friends, describing its relationship with me as being 'complicated'. On the flip side, with adult children scattered around the world, digital connectivity has helped us stay close as a family because we are able to communicate, interact and play across time and space. Playing has been a wonderful feature of technology and it is not discussed enough when we look at family and social lives.

I like to think that I live a socially and culturally rich family and work life, very much enabled by technology. I push technologies to their limits to make them better in the 'mangled practice' of my digital and non-digital life, so that I can be more effective in what I wish to do (my thanks to Will Venters who introduced me to that term!). We often fail to appreciate the satisfaction of organising, categorising and modularising our lives (which I cover in Chapter 7), and I am a hopeless geek in this regard. My own life epitomises deep personalisation of digital technologies and I must admit to a selfish reason for writing this book; I hope it will spur the creation of better offerings I am willing to buy.

Finally, it is impossible for me to cover all of the impacts and activities of the digital economy. I have structured this book somewhat to cover a subset of what I believe is necessary to communicate my points. I have taken from many disciplines, and apologise if I have not done justice to the depth of each. This is not a textbook. It aims to be primarily interesting and only secondarily informative. I hope you may find it helpful for your endeavours.

During the waning days of my doctorate life – which lasted six years and saw the creation and destruction of seven mathematical economic models – my PhD advisor said that I could never be a good theoretical modeller in economics. I saw too many parameters at work. Parsimony would elude me, he said.

I agree completely. In a sense, my years of practice and entrepreneurial activity have 'corrupted' me from pure reductionistic economics. I saw too many connections between concepts, ideas, disciplines, practice and theory, and I could hold many of them together in my head for a long time until it all made sense. As a consequence, my own academic identity, in terms of the discipline to which I belong, escaped me for many years. I have finally decided that if this is what I am, I would let it be an asset, rather than an impediment.

I hope, after reading this book, you will agree.

# Acknowledgements

I am immensely grateful for the generosity of my academic and business colleagues who have helped me with my thinking over the past fifteen years. They have given me ideas, concepts and words, and while I try my best to credit them and their work, I am very sure I have left out many. If I have not acknowledged your work, please contact me and I would be happy to include your reference in the relevant section for the next edition.

I have many to thank. The RCUK NEMODE+ network of academics who have been incredibly generous with ideas, insights and pointers on what I should read, and where I could do more research. My collaborators on the EPSRC SeRTES and EPSRC TEDDI C-Aware grant projects who have helped me think through some of the research questions in this space. My entrepreneurial friends who constantly regale me with tales of industry challenges so that I am forced to think through the relevance of some of my own work, keeping me grounded on making a difference. My managerial colleagues who are untiring in their pursuit of knowledge and their constant mission to change their companies for the better. And the many who have funded my work directly or indirectly.

I give special acknowledgement to the ESRC, EPSRC and RCUK Digital Economy programme who have funded my time and research that helped me think through many of the concepts in this book. I must also thank my Twitter followers and Facebook friends who have been very helpful in providing digital stories and cases to illustrate this book.

More specifically, my thanks go to Yin F Lim, a dear friend whom, after twenty-two years, has learnt to tolerate my idiosyncrasies much more than any production editor should need to; David Brunnen, whose style editing helped make this book much more readable than when I first wrote it; Sarahjane Jones, who helped with references, and Laura Smith who journeyed with me over the last four years on my research in value and service; my academic friends Roger Maull and Steve Vargo – I somehow think better when I talk to the both of you; my daughter Elizabeth whose artistic abilities in creating the comic illustrations in the book helped lighten the mood; my other two daughters Samantha and Serene for distracting me out of my slow days just by insisting I talk to them. Finally, my husband Boon Ho who spoilt me with so much support, care and food that I feel I really should write another book.

# 1 Introduction and impact of digitisation on markets

Nobel prize-winning scientist Dr Arno Penzias marked his retirement in 1995 with a slim volume, *Harmony*, in which he reduced the history of technological development to three eras – making things (the industrial revolution), making things that work (the post-war quality revolution) and making things that work *with* other things, for which he chose the label 'harmony for the information' revolution.

Recognition of the digital economy came about in the late 1990s, emerging from Nicholas Negroponte's observation of a movement away from processing material (manufacturing economy) to processing bits (information economy) (Negroponte, 1995). The term 'digital economy' was popularised by Don Tapscott's book of the same name (Tapscott, 1997), principally to describe how the Internet would change society and business. Both Negroponte and Tapscott discussed how this new economy of connectivity and content enabled by technological developments would create very different opportunities for businesses and people to gather information, interact, communicate and collaborate.

The technologies that were evident two decades ago were by today's standards, a fairly primitive mix. The components have now been untangled and developed separately, but the dominant ambition throughout has been a struggle for 'interoperability'. We can now see how that spirit of technological interoperability impacts on markets across all sectors of the economy. Music is a case in point.

In 2011, digital music sales surpassed CD and record sales for the first time. Global revenues for record companies grew by an estimated 8 per cent to US\$5.2 billion in 2011, with subscription services being the fastest expanding sector. According to the International Federation of the Phonographic Industry (IFPI), the number of users paying to subscribe to a music service increased 65 per cent in 2011 to 13.4 million globally, even while music piracy is still rampant (IFPI, 2012). Yet, overall music sales have dropped by half since companies saw record sales of music (through CDs) back in 1999.

With free music provision from Spotify, Internet radios, social networks and YouTube, today's music consumer has more choice of channels than ever before, and with rampant piracy, many have opted not to pay at all. The example of digital music usefully illustrates many aspects of the creative disruption that is now impacting the entire economy.

Music, as an offering, is in the more advanced stages of digitisation, to the extent that the change to a digitised form has impacted its nature, something I call *digital backwash*. Digital backwash is when the act of digitising an offering fundamentally requires a rethink of how the offering itself has to change. This is also the case with books, for example. When books became electronically available as e-books, it was clear that the book could be much more than its material version. You could now increase the font size if the print was too small; you could tap on a word and a little pop-up window would tell you its meaning. All of these new ways of interacting with the book came about as a result of digitising the material book. Similarly, in the case of music, its content can be changed and mixed in such a way that the medium and the message are almost functioning as one; take, for example, listening to music on MTV.

While many have analysed these cases from strategic and innovation perspectives, this book will take the perspective of the individual's use and value of offerings (such as photographs and music), and the changing nature of markets as a result of digitisation.

Since Theodore Levitt published *Marketing Myopia*, marketing folks have been promoting and marketing offerings based on the benefits a product gives to an individual. The way the marketing folks tell it is that it's not about drills, but the holes in the walls that customers want; not cars but transportation (and/or status); not TV but entertainment. This is of course true. People buy products and services not for the offerings themselves, but for what they can do for them.

Yet, while marketing diligently persuades you to buy for the benefits, the revenues derived from these offerings are *not aligned* to the benefits. You do not *pay* for holes in walls, for example, nor do you *pay* for each trip in your car or whenever you watch your TV. What you do pay for is ownership. Through ownership, you will obtain availability of the car, TV and drill for you to derive the benefits whenever you want them. In the past, the use of offerings could only be possible through ownership, even if it was conditional and temporal ownership such as with car leasing and renting DVDs or TVs.

As technological interoperability advances and markets refashion themselves to exploit new opportunities, it is now becoming increasingly evident that for some products at least, you may be able to get the usage benefits on demand and without even partial ownership. Instead, you could buy into the 'affordance' of a product, i.e., what it enables you to achieve.

## EVOLUTION OF MUSIC TO MEDIA CONTENT AS A CASE STUDY

Music is a case in point. It used to be that you had to acquire a CD or a record before you could listen to it. That means you must buy, own, lease and then use. If you felt like listening to some classical music, for example, you would need to go to the shop to get a CD, if you didn't have one. If you turn that thought on its head, we buy almost everything before we use it, so we must imagine, project and plan the objects we wish to have before we use them. Not surprising that, except for variety in brands, we buy much of the same stuff over and over again because we know we need them and they work.

With digitisation, offerings such as music can now sit at 'virtual' locations such as in the cloud,[1] and you only need a device such as your computer or your mobile phone with broadband/Wi-Fi or 3G connection to access these locations and stream the music for you to listen to it. This brings the availability of music to wherever and whenever you want it,

---

[1] www.thecloud.net/. Accessed 15 November 2012.

i.e., *in context*, which is when the need is most salient, and *on demand*. You may still need to pay for it, but you can now do so whenever you want, rather than having to buy before or after the need arises. For an offering such as music, buying and using can collapse into the same context of time and space. This convergence between buy and use, enabled by digitisation, has seen four major market effects:

- **Serving the unserved market**. First, when buying and using are separated in time, a large part of potential demand is unrealised. Say you wish to listen to classical music and you do not have the CD. You are at home and so you might not buy it until later, when the moment of need has passed or been forgotten. The separation of time from when we buy to when we use means that needs are unfulfilled and they become latent. Latent needs create what I call the 'unserved market', or what economists would call 'latent demand'. This demand is invisible. After all, does McDonald's know how many people walk away when the queues are too long?

- While our latency does not manifest in demand for the firm, it also leaves us rather dissatisfied. When we do want something, we clearly only have access to the things we have bought. In a world of heady consumerism where much has been said about how we are spoilt for choice in terms of products and services, it is ironic that the only choice of coffee we have when we wake up in the morning is the one that is in our kitchen cupboard.

- **Choice of access and ownership**. The second impact of convergence is the possibility to gain use and benefits without ownership but just through access. Since music is now digitised, you could listen to it without owning it. You may still need to pay for it though – but through other means, e.g., you could stream music for free but be subjected to ads as in the case of Spotify. Digital access to music gives you the benefits wherever and whenever you want them, without a long separation of time between buy and use. Of course there will be many who still wish to own their music and you can often buy, own and use without a time separation as well. In fact, by giving people a *choice* of ownership and access, the market expands. If access was cheaper than ownership, the needs of those who originally could not afford to buy CDs, and the rest of the unserved market, would be addressed.

- **New use contexts**. The third impact of convergence is the creation of new use contexts. Where previously music was just for your own listening pleasure, its availability wherever and whenever you want it has made it possible for music to be shared, shown or showcased in different ways for different reasons. Now you can use it to check lyrics, challenge your friends on the year it was released, or share your mood with others on a social network through your choice of song. Music is now not just for listening pleasure, but is also a resource for socialisation.

- **Change in the offering's content – beyond music**. Digitisation of music and its new use contexts has created a demand for audio content that is social, informational and even educational, wherever and whenever you wish to listen to it. This has spawned a market for creating new audio and video content. You can now have audio content to coach your running, and in combination with a GPS, get a guided tour of the city. Some of this content is professionally made but much of it is user-generated, such as mashups and ways to change and splice different types of music into a changed offering. In the UK in 2012, the Deputy Prime Minister, Nick Clegg's apology for a policy u-turn was remixed into a 'sorry song' that went viral. The 'sorry song' then became available on iTunes with purchases contributing to his nominated charity. The idea that no content is sacred, and the possibility of any audio content being combined with other types of content such as audio books and lectures suggests the entry of other industries, legal framework notwithstanding. Through digitisation, an iPod with a podcast could potentially disrupt the education industry. This trend is set to continue, challenging market boundaries of existing firms.

These four major market effects have served to grow the potential market of music into its general form, i.e., media content with a ready and willing market of media content users. I say 'potential' because not all of the media content currently being experienced or used is paid for in a direct way. Piracy aside, media content is often streamed 'free' through YouTube, last.fm and Spotify in exchange for ad views. Direct sales of content therefore account only for a fraction of the content accessed and experienced. Regardless of the challenges in monetising music use and experience, music sales as a whole increased between 3 January 2011 and 1 January 2012 by 6.9 per cent compared to the previous year.[2]

Not everyone buys into access as an offering though, and you can imagine why. Before it was fully digitised, the purchase of a CD meant unlimited access to the music purchased. No one could tell you whom you could lend it to, where you could keep it, who listened to it and how many times you could listen to it. Of course, it also meant that it could only be listened to in one context at a time (you could not lend it to someone and still have access to it, unless you illegally cloned it). With digitised virtual music becoming an accessible rather than an owned offering, music has liberated itself from its physical form and in doing so, become much more shareable. Music licensees, alarmed by the loss of revenue, have started to restrict such activities. By doing this, the market has divided itself into those who prefer ownership (and unlimited access) and those who could do without ownership, with a range of trade-off markets in between.

## THE NEW BATTLEGROUND IN DIGITISATION

Offering digitised media content that is enjoyable and shareable, however, requires three further service provisions:

- Content must reach the customer through a medium from which the customer is able to listen, watch or interact: e.g., an iPod, a computer, a TV or a mobile phone.
- For content to be accessible in context, there must be connectivity.

---

[2] www.businesswire.com/news/home/20120105005547/en/Nielsen-Company-Billboard%E2%80%99s-2011-Music-Industry-Report. Accessed 23 November 2012.

- With content increasingly becoming a shareable resource, the platform for social connectivity to others is becoming a growing priority for media content users.

It is clear now that with greater connectivity between people and things, the biggest land grab for markets of the future is playing out in your living room, while you exercise at the gym, or live your life commuting to work, play and home. Digitisation can make widgets such as smartphones and tablets more personal than ever before if they are enabled by content and connectivity, to serve you better in context (see Figure 1.1). Or you could say that *content* becomes more personal in serving you, enabled by connectivity and widgets, depending on whose point of view is in the land grab.

The perspectives matter because each embodies the giants in each industry. In media, large corporations are competing with peta-bytes of user-generated content on YouTube. With such content, you can learn how to cook a Spanish omelette and repair your phone, often for free. This competes with industry stalwarts who are eager to charge for more formal and professionally created content.

The connectivity industry includes the big broadband providers, 3G and 4G, with near-field communication, fibre, auto-Ids and sensor

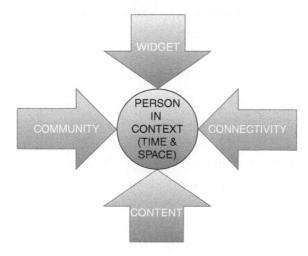

FIGURE 1.1: The future battleground for service in context

technologies all coming to play in the same space. The rise of social platforms such as Facebook, Instagram and Foursquare demonstrate that the social space also holds sizeable influence over the way we live our lives. And of course, we mustn't forget the manufacturers who are creating widgets, big and small, and which are increasingly looking to be connected – from cars, fridges, buildings, to a simple watch, bag and even tables, mirrors and household furniture.

All these major industries are now playing in the new battle-ground of *service in context* – the context in which you go to work, watch your programmes, look after your children and even make your tea or coffee in the morning. This is because even if we are completely unique people, our actions and activities in the contexts of experiencing things (products) are often very similar across many people. I call these *contextual invariances* or *contextual archetypes*, and they are social contexts such as tea-making, commuting to work and keeping grandparents updated about their grandchild.

There are many perspectives and much more interoperability within these new blends of context archetypes. The personal context at the core of these new blends is a response to:

- the capacity of their connectivity;
- the functionality of their devices and networked services;
- the processing power and ease of use of available content and Applications (apps); and
- the impact on the way we live within various communities.

These contexts are rich in meaning and reveal how we want to live our lives. Greater visibility or awareness of these contextual archetypes would enable firms to design future offerings to serve you right within the time and space of these contexts. Yet, these contexts are 'messy', dynamic and may involve millions of inter-actions which makes it hard to understand and draw insights from.

If digitisation, and thus the ability to generate data out of contextual lives, is considered the 'new oil' as some have suggested, context is now the new oil field, with industries trying their best to control territories to drill for the new oil. Yet this new oil is elusive. Data can, at best, capture only part of our lived lives, e.g., the food we bought, perhaps even what we ate, how we travelled, the miles we ran, the photos we kept or the nuances of our interactions on social networks.

However, as devices and things become more able to measure how we live our lives, the picture becomes clearer, even to ourselves. Since these measurements and devices give us greater visibility of ourselves, they often enable us to change what we might normally do. If you knew that your knee problem was possibly related to the fact that you walk 2.5 km every day just within your home, you may decide to change the way you move around the house.

What this means is that every individual person can take advantage (or not) of all this new information to change or make their lives better, in a way that would better suit them. Yet, even while more of our lived lives are now visible and measurable, it raises the question of who holds that data and all the privacy issues related to it. Companies would like to have some of that data so that they can offer more services in context, but would we want them to?

Offerings that change the way we live our lives aren't at all new. We have been changing our lives quite a bit over time, such as choosing low-fat milk or wholemeal bread for a healthier lifestyle, but we've done so with less digital visibility because there wasn't much accessible data or information about us and how we live our lives. Much of these daily life changes come from adapting our lives around the stuff we acquire. And we have acquired quite a lot of it. Chris Techmire[3] who is aged over thirty and married with a son counted that his family has 3,377 items. That is a lot of stuff.

---

[3] www.simplefamilyfinance.com/experiments-in-frugality-1-final-update/. Accessed 15 November 2012.

Where do all these things come from? We bought many of them. Or someone else did and gave them to us. Somehow, somewhere along the way, that bag becomes important for holding things, this bottle for carrying water, that mug to drink coffee from, the pens to write with, the phone to receive text messages, the desk for writing on, the chair to sit on while writing on that desk, and the well-fitting clothes that make us comfortable.

As a result, it isn't surprising that our inventory is above 1,500 objects per person, without counting perishables such as food and drink. Human beings are clever, resourceful creatures. Each and every object we use has been acquired as a resource to help us solve a problem, and by doing so, potentially make our lives better. Every object therefore potentially fulfils a need. Every object is potentially a resource towards helping us achieve something we would otherwise not be able to do, or would perform poorly. Humans have become cleverer at solving problems with different offerings, at living our lives more efficiently and effectively. We are tooled and resourced up, empowered to do much more than we could ever achieve before. We also buy stuff because it is part of 'us' and our identity; it says something about who we are. We also waste much of what we buy, which is why buying efficiency is also a key driver to new markets.

Where is all this going and what does the future hold? Are our lives all about accumulating even more stuff? You might have noticed that I said every object that we buy is *potentially* a resource. I say 'potential' because even if the object has been purchased and it exists in your home or office, it does not mean it immediately fulfils a need. You might *think* it does, but to actually do so, it must be *used* or *experienced*. This is not a trivial point. We have many objects we have bought but do not use because (a) we lent them to someone, (b) we forgot where we put them, or (c) we are in one place and the objects are somewhere else (think of the umbrella you left at home when it rains while you are out).

This brings us back to the point I made earlier, that owning something is not enough. That object must be accessible as and when we want it. So how can we make 1,500 objects accessible in context and on demand? We could try lugging around 1,500 objects but clearly that is impractical. We also don't need all of them all of the time, so some things can be kept at home, and some in the office. As we become more mobile and liberated to do different things at different locations however, this might become problematic. So might we really like to converge some of that stuff to still have the functional use of 1,500 objects but carry less?

I'd like to speculate that we will own less because a lot of our stuff is becoming *connected*, *smart* and *multifunctional*. Connectivity is beginning to reduce the amount of stuff we own. For example, we no longer need to buy an alarm clock, because our mobile phones could serve as one. In fact, something as ubiquitous as the mobile phone is becoming a substitute for much of the 'stuff' we need; a camera, a calculator, a radio, even an entertainment centre. Access to the Internet has reduced the need for dictionaries and encyclopaedias. This is the result of what technologists call 'technological convergence', where interoperable systems and devices are beginning to converge to allow for multiple tasks – often eclipsing their original design purposes. Is this a mobile phone in my hand or is it a remote control for my digital music library?

What is driving convergence in the industrial space? There are two market-driven reasons for firms to move towards convergence:

- First, as a firm, you get immediate access to both markets when you converge two offerings. If there is an affordability issue, merging both markets means saving the customer money, i.e. two offerings for the price of one. Fewer people tend to buy regular cameras now, since cameras on phones have become commonplace and able to take the decent high-resolution photos. Camera phones are now outselling digital cameras to a ratio of 6:1.[4]

---

[4] Camera phones with 3 MP and bigger sensors outsold digital still cameras 6:1 in 2012 (www.unwiredview.com, posted on 19 December 2012). Accessed 20 December 2012.

- Second, as a firm, you are also able to pre-empt others from taking away your existing market because you create a differentiated product. Objects of the future, therefore, will tend to converge rather than diverge.
- Third, technology is now able to combine the digital and the material. Products can now be created as 'open' rather than fixed products, allowing customers to configure and personalise them to their changing circumstances of use, e.g., the smartphone (Yoo et al., 2012).

Yet it may not be so straightforward. Before the sustainability and minimalist folks out there get too carried away, celebrating that we will be reducing the quantity of things we buy, we may still be accumulating more things. This is because many of the things we buy are actually our way of mitigating the risks of not having them when we want them. Think of the things you need most at the time you need them (such as toilet paper, water, food) and you will realise that we will always buy them in advance.

In the same way, we only need to feel uncertain about an object's availability to spur us to buy early, and sometimes buy more. Another reason why objects may not converge is because choice is reduced. We may not like the camera that is on our phone because we would prefer a more powerful camera. By the same token, some households prefer to have a separate dryer from a washing machine rather than a combined one because it is not possible to use the washing machine when someone is using it for drying. The key issue is to understand why, how and when we acquire, engineer and experience the resources we need to live our lives.

The way we are communicating, creating, learning and inter-acting today is changing all the time because technology helps us to create bigger networks, and allows us to access larger connected spaces and virtual communities. Because of digital technologies, things are transforming into different forms. The book is now a Kindle, the watch a heart-rate monitor, the DVD player a GameBox connected with gamers around the world, the TV a news feed and communication device. The list is endless.

The question then becomes one of understanding and prescribing the way forward. How do we understand ways to design connected offerings of the future? Are there methodologies for market development? Is everyone shooting in the dark and just hoping that there is a market for this newfangled thing that they have just developed? Are we creating technological solutions that are in search of problems? Is there a way of understanding how contexts of use in human lives could be best served by future widgets, connectivity, social platforms and content?

This book seeks to probe these questions and provide a better understanding of the opportunities. In Chapter 2, I will begin with something that is fundamental to our understanding; what we consider as 'value'.

## CHAPTER I REFLECTIONS

In this chapter we've reviewed the origins of what is now called the digital economy and how the impacts of digitisation are enabling fresh approaches to the design and delivery of almost everything.

Some impacts – in music and photography – have been relatively easy to realise but they provide useful clues for future designs.

The old boundaries between a product and the way it is used are shifting – and with those shifts come new insights into what we, the customers, may regard as valuable.

It is in understanding the new dynamics of individual contexts and the greater flexibility for adaptation that firms must now envisage the development of their products and services.

But to make sense of this whirlwind of digitally-enabled dimensions, we should first step back and consider what is meant by value.

# 2   Back to basics – what is value?

Value is an elusive concept. As a term, it has been so overused and abused that any attempt to define it seems to encounter disagreement from every quarter. Yet even if the understanding of value is diverse, we 'get it' in a rather colloquial way. We might not agree on the precise definition of value, but that disagreement is often at the margins of the way we bound it in terms of what it is and what it is not.

So let me start by saying that this book is one person's view of value – mine. While it is my view, it is grounded on some ten years of thinking and research – not just my research alone, but that of many other eminent scholars. Over the course of the book, I hope to persuade you that this view, slowly being accepted by many others in practice and academia, is actually quite useful in helping you glean some insights into what is happening in the world. Hopefully, it also offers a way forward in terms of thinking about innovation and the creation of new markets.

If I say that 'something that is of value is usually something good', this statement would usually receive some broad agreement, even though we might perhaps argue about what goodness means. So let's start with just that. Goodness.

Of course if you are from a business or economics discipline, you might immediately think – no, that is not the value that businesses and governments talk about, but I will ask you to bear with me as I attempt to connect the dots. It may not seem important, but I do think it is.

Businesses and governments today may not necessarily think of value as 'goodness', but there is actually a historical basis for doing so. The notion of 'good', and what we think is 'good' about ourselves, is embedded in our values, i.e., the beliefs that we hold most dear, that guide our thoughts and behaviour. Our values reside deep in our subconscious, and whether or not we are fully aware of them, they govern the way we act, the choices we make and the friends we have.

Over time, the term 'value' began to hold two types of meaning: the goodness of ourselves embedded within our values, and the goodness of others – be they people, ideas, products, activities or anything physical that is external to ourselves. The latter is the focus of this book.

I'm not yet done with the history though.

## ATOMISTIC VALUE

Value has been discussed by philosophers as far back as over 2,000 years ago. Plato first suggested that there are two types of value: extrinsic and intrinsic (Cross & Woosley, 1964). According to Plato, something that has extrinsic value is good to have because it can help us do something with it, i.e., it is instrumental for something else. Something that is intrinsic is good to have for itself. Plato suggested that these two types of value are not mutually exclusive; some things in life have both extrinsic and intrinsic value. For example, a mug can be used for drinking (extrinsic), or because it is pretty or has sentimental value, it can be good to have for itself (intrinsic). You can now think about the mug as having 'properties' that are of value.

More than 2,000 years later (I don't know why they took so long), Dewey (1949) suggested that the extrinsic and intrinsic value of something depends on

the situation and the context. Basically, when situations change, the extrinsic or intrinsic properties of the object also change. The mug on an office desk may have more extrinsic value than the same mug on a shelf.

A whole academic school of thought has evolved from 'value', called *axiology*. It is devoted to the philosophical study of value, and is concerned with the analysis of value, its frameworks and the evaluation of what is 'valuable', or with the assignment of value to items, properties or states.

One such philosopher, G.E. Moore (1993), suggested that the nature of goodness (value) cannot be a natural property. In other words, if the goodness of something is its 'essence', that goodness cannot be naturally occurring. So a description of an object, an event or anything else can only be good if it is perceived to be so by an individual who will be realising its goodness. 'Goodness' can therefore only be subjectively evaluated. The intrinsic or extrinsic properties of a mug are now not its natural properties; these are bestowed upon the mug by the person perceiving it.

Of course, a mug could have characteristics that will result in many people perceiving it as good. For example, the handle of the mug is good because you can hold it and most people would agree and perceive that as good. Similarly, an ice cream on a hot day is deemed 'good' because a perceiver attributes goodness to it, and not necessarily because the ice cream is naturally good.

Scholars developing thoughts around value have tried ways of classifying extrinsic or intrinsic value. Some have suggested that intrinsic value is like an emotional dimension of value, while extrinsic value could have practical and logical dimensions (Mattsson,

1992). So a chair has the practical dimension of a 'seat' and has the logical dimension of 'width, size or height', but could also have some emotional dimension of being 'great-grandpa's chair', all of which contribute to the

individual's perception of why the chair is 'good' or valuable to him. Others such as Hartman (1967) propose a further dimension – that of 'systemic value' – where the characteristics of the object that is good is defined by a system, or the norm. For example, a chair is only good if it can seat a person without falling over, since all good chairs share the same property.

Such a way of looking at value makes a big assumption. It assumes that value is an 'essence' of an object. Yes, it may subjectively be perceived differently by different people, but such perceptions are the subjective perceptions of the essence. It doesn't change the fact that fundamentally, those who subscribe to this view (called *atomistic* value) believe that anything of value must have an 'essence of goodness' within it, even if this is subjectively bestowed upon it.

## PHENOMENOLOGICAL VALUE

Between 1929 and 1939, two influential philosophers, Heidegger and Husserl, came up with a different philosophical proposition that had an impact on how we think about value. I am not about to launch into phenomenology or existentialism here. However, Husserl did suggest that individuals conceive objects through their experiences of them, i.e., the interaction between the object and the individual (Husserl, 1939).

This means that the value of an object such as a mug arises from a person's experience, interaction or relationship with that mug. It is not the 'essence' of the mug that is of value. Value is *created*

only when the mug is experienced in some way. This means that in atomistic value, value is an essence that sits within the mug but for phenomenological value, the mug has no value at all until it is being acted upon or interacted with.

Thinking about value in this way means that the value in objects is not just the object itself. Why would you value a mug? Is it because the mug is part of your daily life and practices? It implies that the mug has meaning only because your life has meaning, and your life has meaning only when you act.

This is Heidegger's existential philosophy, where he considers the meaning of human existence as dependent on how we achieve our own 'projects' in our daily lives (Heidegger, 1996/1927). This means that the goodness of objects (their value) comes from your use and experience of these objects, i.e., the actions to achieve possible projects and to perform practices with these objects (e.g., physically use them or emotionally experience them). And our 'projects' are really very much the way we enact our social and cultural lives.

Bear in mind that the 'use' of these objects, enacted through actions, interactions and relationships between you and the object, may not always be physical. In the case of 'great-grandpa's chair', phenomenological value is created when it is experienced mentally by the individual within his or her consciousness. This is similar in concept to the value of a Ferrari on the driveway. You don't have to use it to value it, because you are emotionally and mentally interacting with it in terms of the pride and status it gives you. The value is emergent and experienced between the object and yourself, in contrast to Hartmann's atomistic view of value, where value lies as an essence within an object, only to be perceived as good by the individual.

I will discuss why the former may be a more useful philosophy to adopt in terms of understanding value for businesses in a digitally connected world. Before I do that though, there is still a bit more of history to go through.

## MONEY CHANGES EVERYTHING

So far we have considered value as something good arising from an object, whether created from the experience of it, or in the essence of it. In the eighteenth century, as nations began to trade and more objects were produced, philosophers, mathematicians and early economists began to speculate on other concepts of value. Instead of thinking about why an object is 'good', they began to discuss objects in terms of what they were *worth*. This was important then because wealth came about from making things that were worth something to some people so that they would buy them.

Soon, value became less about goodness arising from the essence or the experience of the object, and more about what the object could be exchanged for, i.e., its worth. In 1776, Adam Smith wrote *The Wealth of Nations* and discussed 'value-in-use' as the goodness of an object's use, and 'value-in-exchange' as the object's power of purchasing other objects. The intention then was to develop an understanding of the processes or purposes of exchange that contributed to the wealth of Britain at the time – a discipline that later became known as economics (Vargo & Morgan, 2005).

At that time, due to limitations on international travel and lack of communication technologies, the primary source of national wealth was through the production and export of surplus goods. As a result, Smith shifted his emphasis to value-in-exchange and focused on what he deemed

'productive' activities; those that contributed to exchange value through the manufacturing and distribution of tangible goods. That thinking led to the belief that all labour not resulting in units of tangible and exportable output was 'unproductive' (Vargo & Lusch, 2004).

The economic scholars who followed Smith generally disagreed with his classifications (Say, 1821) and recognised that all activities that contributed to well-being were productive (had value-in-use). But Smith's model of value embedded and distributed in tangible goods fits well with the increasing desire to turn economic philosophy into an economic science. At that time, the model of 'science' was Newtonian Mechanics, the study of matter embedded with properties, and so most scholars came round to accepting Smith's view of productive activities, which was focused on the output of tangible objects.

It became suitable, therefore, to subscribe to atomistic value because the 'essence' of value can then be created from production. Over time, the essence of what is good about an object became its 'utility'. An object is of value because it is embedded with 'utilities' that can be bought or exchanged. This became the focus of neoclassical economics, with goods produced (supply) by firms in exchange for money given by the customer who wants the object to fulfil a need/want.

This in turn creates a market for the object around which trade and commerce have thrived over the past two centuries. Value of any object then evolved into a different description of 'goodness'. It is now goodness in exchange and it has become a central focus of firms and governments. Producing objects with exchange value has therefore made manufacturing the stalwart of economic life since the start of the industrial era. I will call this exchange value *worth*.

The difference between utility and 'use' or value-in-use is important. Utility is concerned with the *buying* of the object, i.e., utility is the unit that drives how we choose: e.g., I choose A over B because A gives me more utility. So the notion of utility does not really concern itself with the *actual* use of the object; it only concerns itself with how useful I *think* it might be at the point of choosing and buying, i.e., during its exchange. So utility is actually a unit for deciding worth. If you subsequently use the object and find it useless (no value-in-use), that is not relevant to utility.

Let's try to understand this more clearly. You might be thinking – if I find that something is good, shouldn't it be exchangeable for something else? So isn't value (the goodness) from use the same as value (goodness) from worth?

Not really. While both value-in-use and worth (value-in-exchange) describe the 'goodness' of something, the former is the goodness from use/experience, while the latter is the goodness for exchange with something else. Let me explain.

Converting something that has value-in-use to worth means a conversion of something useful into an economic value. This is not straightforward, is it? A man with skills in cooking has use-value to himself and his family. Could he use the same skills to become a chef, commodifying his skills into a worth, where a customer could purchase such skills?

By the same token, if an object has worth to you at the point of choice and exchange, it may not be the same as the value you get from the experience. We do this all the time; fruits not eaten, food expired, a piece of equipment used only once. Clearly, the relationship is far more complex. The most important element in between is *the market*. A man with skills to cook can convert those skills for salary (worth) only if there is a market for his skills. Similarly, if you feel you are in need of something, e.g., have value-in-use for a carrot cake, you also need to find a market, a place where you can exchange something (your money) to obtain it.

Using the notion of utility (the perceived usefulness) as a unit of worth has had a severe effect; it has constrained imaginative boundaries, although it is only now with digitisation that we can begin to get a handle on value-in-use.

It used to be that for something to be of value, whether you believed the value was in the essence or in the experience of the object, there had to be a person involved to value it. Using utility as a proxy took away the person involved. Suddenly, objects had value on their own without the need for a 'valuer'.

Firms manufactured things, believing that an object that was good for something has the same goodness anytime anywhere, and that somehow, the value of the object doesn't really need people to value it anymore. It just needed to be produced. The contexts of use and experience are largely ignored. In scientific terms, they were treated as 'exogenous' to the value.

So, an object that was originally thought of as 'good' is now assumed to be all good and always good. This is the world we have built, where stuff such as hammers, printers, furniture, ovens and equipment are all good things that have 'value', but we have forgotten that value comes from their use or experience. All these things (tangible products) are assumed to be 'good' and of value by themselves.

If you start to see it from this perspective, you begin to see how manufacturing has evolved. We make an object that we think is of value (although what we really mean is worth), then we go out to find a market for it. The focus then, is not on *use* or *experience* but on *worth* and *exchange*. In essence, firms and their marketing perspectives became servants to worth. Implicitly, everyone now believes that objects have worth by themselves, without considering how the value is created from these objects.

## GOODS-DOMINANT LOGIC

Once you take this view, you will start to think of value creation as the making of the objects. This then turns production processes into 'value-creating' processes, with the final product holding all the value. And we also begin to think about making these objects 'better' by adding more to the objects, i.e., having more 'functions' means adding value. This is what we call a goods-centric focus, or according to Steve Vargo and Robert Lusch (2004), a goods-dominant logic.

This manner of thinking is deeply entrenched in today's world. We see it in the way we talk about manufacturing and economies.

We discuss 'high value' manufacturing as making objects with 'more functionality' or 'added value attributes' that could convince customers to pay more for them. Goods-dominant logic has driven our economies over the last 200 years. We have developed measurements around it in terms of outputs, and considered what is needed within the economy to make them in terms of skills (counted as labour), capital and technologies.

And let's face it; it has worked. We are better off than we ever were before. Manufacturing has been the stalwart of Western economies for a long time. China rose on the back of manufacturing that moved to the East, so this logic has had a good run. And while it has created a wealthier world, it has also engendered a whole new set of challenges.

I believe there are three other reasons why we choose to cling to the goods-dominant logic. As human beings, we tend to prize what we can see, so it's easy to go down the road of value being tangibly 'inside' something and indeed, in the early 1990s, researchers regarded this as such a dominant design principle that they looked for ways to 'dress up' or 'tangibilise' services to make them comprehensible.

Second, many of the things we use are in contexts and situations *away* from the firm that made them, and *after* the transaction. The way we use the oven, toaster or TV, the way we operate tractors or large equipment – is often *after* the object's production, and the firm has limited visibility of it. Since the data surrounding use and experience, particularly for tangible objects, is scarce or often too complex and costly to access, it has been easier for firms to ignore it. This is especially so since the customer has already bought the item. Unless there is scope for a repeat purchase, why bother?

Finally, since the paymasters of marketing are firms, the natural tendency was for marketing to serve exchange value, rather than use-value, even though marketing is tasked to be customer-centric. While this is the mainstream marketing view, a branch of literature on critical marketing and consumption culture has risen over the past twenty years to champion the individual's use experience (Saren et al., 2007; Schroeder, 2007).

## ENTER THE WORLD OF BUSINESS

Value as exchange or worth has become the default understanding of value in modern times, despite many debates over its definition (Ng & Smith, 2012). Yet, what is wrong with exchange value? Isn't that what commercial life is about? Exchange markets make distribution of production and consumption more efficient, don't they?

Yes, of course. For the past 300 to 400 years, this understanding has worked well, and much economic growth in the nineteenth and twentieth centuries is attributed to it. But something is changing. The way we are 'buying' is slowly changing.

It used to be that we got something for the money we paid. Today, more market offerings are coming to our hands in ways that are not so straightforward. Many of us no longer pay for a phone call. We pay a subscription that allows us to make many phone calls. We also own less of what we use. We stream music and TV shows, we surf the Internet, do virtual banking; many of these activities are not direct exchange activities. They are intangible services rendered through a combination of material and human activities.

I will explain it this way. We've always bought things because we want to use them to make our lives better. So we bought cars to drive ourselves to work, drills to make holes in walls, books to read, CDs to listen to music, cameras to take photos. In purchasing these objects, we

were buying the *potential* to create value so that we could achieve our goals or outcomes.

Yet, while we wanted these benefits and outcomes and thought we were paying for them, we weren't doing so. We were actually paying for ownership of these objects.

Of course by owning something, we get to use it and enjoy the outcomes we want, but that was not what firms saw. They only saw that you paid for ownership, so ownership was how they viewed value. The firms out there making stuff valued you for your purchase of these things and in their minds, ownership was equal to outcomes. After all, how could you possibly get a hole in the wall without a drill?

As technology evolved and digitisation increased, competition drove digital offerings into alternative channels and different business models. We may stop buying CDs because we can now get music wherever we want and in ways that mean we may not even need to own a CD, and indeed, may not even own the music at all. The music industry has witnessed this evolution from ownership of the music to merely listening and accessing the music. This means that two major forces are acting at the same time: the virtualisation/digitisation of the offering (from a CD to just an mp3 file) and the convergence of purchase and use. This means we don't need to buy and then use later, but buy only when we want to use.

Why did this happen? To be honest, ownership is a rather ineffective idea. Think about it. You have to actually think about what you might want as an outcome in the future, and buy the item before you use it. So the cereal, the tea and coffee must be bought and stored in the kitchen before you can use them. If there was a way to buy 'at spot' as the economists would say, it would be much more effective. Certainly, if we didn't need to own some items at all and yet be allowed to just use them, e.g., the drill or the lawn mower, we might prefer it and we wouldn't even need to think about where to store them.

I'm not saying that we don't buy for ownership anymore. The Van Gogh on your wall, or the piece of jewellery on your finger can probably only give you pleasure if you own it; in this case, the 'use' of these items is derived from ownership because it is an emotional type of 'use'. We 'use' them by experiencing a feel-good emotion when we own them.

### BACK TO FIRST PRINCIPLES: A SERVICE-DOMINANT LOGIC

The attachment of the term 'value' to money and worth has been an etymological fascination for me. The term 'value' has always had an effect on people. During one of my seminars at the University of Cambridge where I was fortunate enough to be a visiting scholar for three years, I spoke of value much in the same way I speak of it in this book; that of goodness and its creation. I illustrated the intrinsic notions of goodness, and its innumerability (not able to be measured or numbered) through a tongue-in-cheek analogy of a married couple and the value of a spouse.

My analogy upset one colleague in the audience. After the lecture he proceeded to give me an earful on why his wife would never be considered as 'value'. He saw value as worth and attaching worth to his wife (as if she might be tradable) was deeply offensive. I saw this as another example of our current-day paradigm. I was making the point that etymologically, at least, bringing the term back to its origins of value-in-use might serve to separate value from worth. I would therefore propose that value is the goodness we create out of the experience with something or someone in context, and that experience/interaction is the enactment of our social and cultural values.

Drawing the term 'value' back to its phenomenological origins is important. For one, we currently have no other word to describe

that goodness which we create or experience with people and objects. Calling it *value*, despite its historical baggage, is as appropriate a term as any. Many social scientists, in their effort to humanise a world driven by money, markets and consumption, would probably prefer this definition.

One of the reasons this book proposes to return the definition of value closer to Adam Smith's early reasoning of value-in-use rather than the latter-day value-in-exchange is to help us consider how better to serve future markets.

First, allowing value to be defined only by worth does not sufficiently examine the drivers to that worth. The creation of new markets and innovations must reach further back to why some things are worth a lot while others are not, and why value may not be as consistent as we had thought, because its creation rests in the experience, rather than the ownership or essence, of an item or service.

Second, much of the market economy describes the worth of offerings (and as such, their markets) only after we have seen them. To know what might be useful, and what might be marketable, would require us to think about offerings before they exist and how they might come into existence to begin with. This would give us a way to think about the future, in terms of the latent needs from our day-to-day lives. Understanding value in this manner can help us develop a method for innovation.

Third, offerings are made up of resources put together by firms, be they labour, technology or capital; what I would term as 'input resources'. Yet, in its use, customer resources become essential to fulfil the value proposition (see Chapter 3 on value co-creation). These resources are part of the experience that creates the value, and need to be considered for the design of offerings. Indeed, some of these resources by individuals themselves may become part of the firm's value proposition, especially when they create network effects, which I cover in Chapter 10. This is the case for some offerings such as social networks (Facebook, LinkedIn). In such cases, converting customer resources into a commodity that becomes part of the firm's innovative value proposition may enable us to create new offerings and new markets.

To understand markets of the future therefore, requires an understanding of value in terms of the goodness that individuals create with offerings, rather than in terms of worth. In Chapter 5, commodification and exchanges will be discussed further but first, there is a need to understand more thoroughly phenomenological value creation in a systematic manner if we are to innovate and create new markets for the future.

## CHAPTER 2 REFLECTIONS

In this chapter we have asked what is meant or understood by the multitude of words we use when considering transactions: value, goodness, worth, utility, usefulness, ownership.

Delving into history to untangle these words brings out the distinction between atomistic value which means that value resides in an object as an *essence*, and phenomenological value which means that value resides in the *interaction* between the individual and the object. Take note that in the former, value is created when the object is created. In the latter, value is created only when the object is *experienced* (used).

In the general development of economics, the distinction in these ways of ascribing value may have seemed largely irrelevant and easily ignored in a wealth-creating industrialised world dominated by what is now described as having a 'goods-dominant' logic.

The arrival of digitisation, however, demands that we revisit our understanding of value and accept that 'value is the goodness we create out of the experience with something or someone'. This contextual experience or interaction – this 'value-in-use' or 'value-in-context' – can be described as an enactment of our social and cultural values.

But however we choose to describe it, this shift towards an appreciation of the context in which something is being used has been set free by digitisation. It has escaped from nuanced academic debate into the everyday world of products and services, and the way we live and work. In the next chapter we will delve deeper into this understanding of value and context.

# 3    Value and context

This is how I explain value and context to my students.

I ask them to go to a cafe and evaluate the experience by critically looking at all the attributes (features) of the cafe. They go out, have a nice cup of coffee/tea, and come back after forty-five minutes, notebooks in hand. I ask them to give me the *outcome* of the experience, which I write on the right-hand side of the class whiteboard. I want the emotional and functional outcomes, so they will say 'relaxed', 'feel good', 'caught up with the gossip', 'chilled', 'cosy and warm'.

I then ask them to give me a list of all the attributes of the cafe, which I write on the left side of the board (see Figure 3.1). This part is easy. They usually say 'music', 'ambience', 'good coffee', 'not crowded', 'good seats', 'good heating'. Between the attributes and the outcomes, I create a blank column and I ask them a simple question – how did 'ambience' become 'chilled'? How did 'music' become 'relaxed'? They usually look puzzled, not understanding. Until I say – What if you can't 'hear'? Would 'music' still lead to 'relaxed'? What if you are there to sort out a problem with a boyfriend or girlfriend; would 'ambience' still lead to 'chilled'?

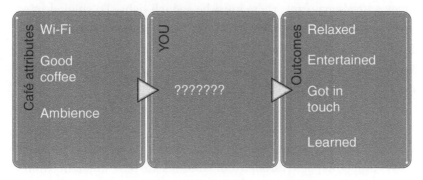

FIGURE 3.1: From attributes to outcomes: the role of the individual

29

They suddenly realise that they have completely forgotten their own role in creating that experience; that they, as customers, co-created value with the cafe. It dawns upon them that for attributes to become outcomes, they have to *realise* the value proposition of the cafe to achieve benefits. And more importantly – and this is a key point – they need to *access their own resources* to co-create that value, whether these resources are their ability to choose the right company with whom to go to the cafe, or even their basic resource of being able to see, hear and feel. *Customers implicitly design themselves and their contexts so that they can co-create value with the firm.*

In essence, it's a lot to do with whether the individual is able to access the resource to achieve his or her outcomes, and whether the firm takes for granted what the customer is able to access. So the best value proposition in the world, say the latest iPhone, is useless if you don't know how to use it. But you could create a lot of value if you did. You may say – isn't this about educating your customer on how to use your product? It may be – for some resources. For example, yes, it is about educating your customer if you want them to understand how to use your washing machine, but the education is basically a means towards giving your customer the right type of skills and competencies (develop their resources) to use your product. So these skills and competencies are one type of resources needed to co-create value.

There are other resources that the customer needs to co-create value that cannot be acquired through education. For example, to enjoy a lovely painting, there must be enough light. To enjoy driving your new sports car, it would be nice to have miles of highway with little traffic. In other words, resources to co-create value are contextually driven. In addition, objects are rarely used on their own, but with other objects or other people in context.

Individuals therefore sit at the hub of many potential resources and integrate them to live their lives better. We are ingenious and dynamic beings who constantly integrate resources and are able to make things happen through our abilities to pull different things together. When a projector is not working well, we know how to put two books at its base and prop it up to improve its projection. We appropriate resources – objects, skills of others – to get the outcomes we want. Christensen and Raynor (2003) call this 'customer jobs'. In that sense, the human individual is the most amazing and dynamic central processing unit – we make things happen by creating connectivity between objects, *through ourselves*, to achieve many varied outcomes throughout the day, week, month and year.

*So value is co-created between the individual and the firm that produces the objects at the point of use, and value is created through resource integration to achieve outcomes, in a context that is designed by the customer.* Let's delve a little deeper into some of these outcomes.

## VALUE-CREATING OUTCOMES

This is how I make a distinction between value and outcomes. Value is the goodness created out of the experience of something, but outcomes are why the object is of value, i.e., outcome is the benefit arising from that goodness. So when we think of something as having value, we can think of it as being 'good' and then discuss why it is so. For example, a phone could be of value because it helps me make a call to check if my daughter has arrived home safely. The phone call made the phone 'good' (of value), but the feeling you got after you made the call is its outcome.

Creating value however, comes from the experience, interaction or use of something. Outcomes, whether positive or negative, come from whether value has been created from the interaction. Given such a definition, there is therefore no such thing as destroying value. You can't destroy something if you've never created it. Instead, if you interact with something and have a negative experience – e.g., you are trying out a new shaver and it gives you a slight electric shock – you create no value with it and this could result in a negative outcome.

The idea of 'use' or 'experience' isn't restricted only to functional use, however. A few years ago, I visited my sister in New York for a month. During my visit, I used my mobile phone with the Wi-Fi

in her home and rarely used the data-roaming service provided by my UK telco. However, I had forgotten to turn off the phone's auto data-roaming function, so when I got slapped with a £560 bill, I was seriously annoyed. I didn't use the service at all and I had to pay for it! What I didn't realise of course, was that I was 'using' the service. Let me explain.

When we consider the word 'use', we immediately think of physical use like using a car, a stove or a TV when actually, the word 'use' has a much broader meaning. Similarly, the word 'consumption' causes us to conjure images of using something, but it means more than that. A Ferrari sitting on your driveway gives you value even if you are not driving it. This is because you are still experiencing the Ferrari on your driveway in the way you derive the status and pride from owning it. So the outcomes arising from value 'in-use' are not merely functional, but also emotional. A piece of art or antique on your mantelpiece gives you great pleasure. Such a pleasure is still value-in-use, because you experience it every time you look at the item.

It gets a bit more complicated and less obvious with certain offerings. In the case of my telco service, I did not 'use' the data service in New York as I was utilising the house Wi-Fi. Yet, one can argue that I did 'use' it, because the mere provision of availability-for-use by the telco is part of the offering. In this case, one must differentiate between the value from actual *use* of the service, and the value from the *availability* of the service. In the former, my outcome is communication and getting information. In the latter, my outcome is assurance and security.

Let's try another example. In my work with the equipment industry, I've noticed that one of the most-used words in maintenance and service contracts is 'availability'; e.g., delivering 95 per cent availability of an engine, or some other equipment. If I were to promise you the availability of a piece of equipment, it doesn't matter whether or not you use it – my job is to make sure that all the parts are in good condition and the equipment works 95 per cent of the time. Of course, you can only hope that the remaining 5 per cent is at a time when it's least critical.

The way you 'use' something would affect its availability, of course. So if you 'use' it badly, the parts would fail more often, requiring more frequent repairs and threatening its availability. The point I'm trying to make here though is that as a customer, availability-for-use is of value, even if I don't actually use it. In my case, even though there was availability of data-roaming service on my mobile phone, it did not really create any value for me since I already had the alternative of the house Wi-Fi. Nonetheless, the telco can still argue that the service of 'availability for assurance' was provided and 'used', because I did not turn off the phone's auto data-roaming function. I have no intention of educating my telco about this – I only asked for my money back since I did not use the service, and they did eventually give me a refund.

If you are still not convinced, think about the servicing and support of a nuclear weapon to achieve value-in-use for the customer. It is the availability-for-use and availability-as-deterrent that is valued and paid for. We all hope it would never actually be used.

'Use' is therefore a misleading term to describe value created in use. We often think about 'use' as some sort of functional use when it is much more than that. I prefer the term 'experiential use', as it denotes both the functional and the emotional aspects of use arising from the aesthetics or symbolism of an object, or other experiences with it.

If you don't believe in experiential use outcomes, take a look at your watch. If it's worth anything more than £10, you bought it for an outcome that is not all functional. If you truly bought a watch for functional outcomes only, you wouldn't pay anything above £10 because a cheap, non-branded quartz watch would work just as well to tell time. If however, you insist that you bought the watch because it is reliable, then you are already buying it for an emotional outcome; you believe that the brand gives you greater reliability.

Think of a chair, whose functional value is the seat with which you co-create value when you sit on it. The attributes of the chair that allow you to create that value and achieve the seat's functional outcome are that which is logical – the chair must be of the right height and it shouldn't fall over when sat upon. These attributes are designed by the manufacturer with their own resources and are familiar to us.

However, emotional outcomes do not depend only on the manufacturer's resources. They depend on our beliefs; the way we believe in a particular brand's promise and, by believing and experiencing it post-purchase, we create meaning for ourselves. So a combination of functional and emotional outcomes is the combination of the firm's and the customer's resources in creating value that is of both meanings – driven and functional.

The firm does contribute to the creation of meanings, of course. This is why so much of a firm's spending goes into communicating the aesthetics, branding and symbols of a product. In the way that a handbag is beautifully produced to achieve a functional outcome, it is also promoted through branding in such a way that it would achieve a meanings-driven emotional outcome with your own emotional resources and beliefs.

Yet, much of what I have discussed is only the role of the customer and the firm in co-creating value. The actual value (co-) creation occurs in context, i.e., where and when it actually happens. This means we need to understand the time and space of contexts.

Let's go back to the mug. We've established that we are taking the position that value is co-created through the experience of the mug. So value is subjective – not in our perception of the essence of the mug, but through our experiential use of it. What this means is that the value you create whenever you use the mug is an experiential event unique to you.

So now we can say that on a planet of six billion people with each using a mug every day, their individual experiences will create many different 'values in context'. This is a long (and possibly discomforting) way from the notion of a relatively stable exchange value for the mug.

Now that doesn't mean that there are no similarities between how we experience a mug. Just because the value is unique or different doesn't mean that we can't think of the *context* of the experience as exhibiting some sort of pattern or consistency, or what I would label as *invariance* across experiences.

## CONTEXT: THE NEW FOCUS FOR VALUE CREATION

Context is the time and space of experiential use. It includes the environment, people and objects, and more importantly, it is based on the perspective of the individual. Explaining context is best done through the story of the camera.

On 19 January 2012, Eastman Kodak US filed for bankruptcy protection. An iconic firm formed in 1889 by George Eastman, Kodak dominated the photographic film business for more than a hundred years. During its heyday in 1976, it commanded 90 per cent of film sales and 85 per cent of camera sales in the US (Gavetti et al., 2005).

What happened? Hundreds of business school students and numerous newspapers, magazines and journals have described and analysed the Kodak failure, with many concluding that Kodak did not move quickly enough into the digital era even though the digital camera was invented by Steven Sasson, a Kodak engineer. Kodak's dallying for fear of cannibalising its film business resulted in competitor Canon seizing a sizeable market share.

The subsequent ubiquity of camera phones created further problems. Urban legend has it that a well-known business consultancy commissioned by Kodak to research into the future of photographs around the turn of the century, when approximately 86 billion

analogue photographs were taken per annum, reported that only one in ten photographs printed were shared. The rest were left gathering dust in photo albums. So it was concluded that the future of photographs would probably not be in the direction of shareability. Imagine the surprise when, within ten years by 2010, the number of photos shared online is 11 billion and rising, with experts predicting that the numbers will double by 2015. The number of photographs taken have also soared, with some studies estimating the total number to be around 380 billion. Printing photos at home and in store has dropped to a third at 27 billion.

How do we explain this? The digital revolution of photography is a case in point on the power of digitisation to change both the message (what photos are taken) as well as the medium (the channels for taking the photos and for communication and sharing). Where we used to take photographs for memories, the ability now to generate (and erase) a photo on demand means that photographs could be taken for many reasons without incurring any further economic costs. Today, photographs are no longer just for keeping memories but for collecting evidence after an accident, or photographing a notice or telephone number when there is no pen or paper. The most obscure use I have recently heard of was to take a picture of an injury on a person's back where the person couldn't see the injury directly.

Since we now have the ability to share a photo without needing to print it, we can now share for different reasons. Last week, I took photos of handbags in a store to share on Facebook so that my daughter could see them and choose the one she wanted. My second daughter just called to ask me to take a picture of the kettle in the house because she was trying to convince her father that the kettle they were both looking to buy at the store was of the same colour as the one at home. Humorous photos have become *memes* – units that carry cultural ideas, symbols and practices virally on social networks – creating communities of common purposes, for play and fun.

The consultancy engaged by Kodak over ten years ago didn't get it wrong. It was probably true that only one in ten photographs were shared before photos were digitised; it's just that the sharing mechanism was through a printed medium. Today, freed from the need to be printed, photographs and other images have become social resources on steroids. The photograph as an offering has completely changed in terms of its benefits, its content and its channels, from creating it to communicating it. To me, this is extreme digital backwash.

Digitisation has had a further effect that is subtle, but very important to the understanding of value created in context. Having a camera on a mobile phone isn't just about a different type of camera, but about the fact that the mobile phone gives a camera greater mobility and easier interoperability between our different social contexts.

Some of you may remember the first time the mobile phone came with a camera. Were you one of those who said: 'Now why would I want a camera on my phone?' I certainly was. Why did its use become so popular? Because by giving the camera greater mobility, it is always with you. It became *present. In context. On demand.* At the moment when you most need it. As opposed to your 'real' camera which is probably sitting in a drawer somewhere at home. This has an important implication for the creation of new markets.

**Context is where the willingness to pay (and therefore worth) could be highest.** An offering that is able to serve context on demand, is able to be present 'where the money is'. Think about the time you really needed something, such as a plaster for a wound. The ability to

Uh.. the button's popped. I'd pay you good money for a safety pin right now.

serve context is where both revenues (for firms) and need (for customers) are aligned, creating a win-win situation and usually, a higher willingness to pay from the customer's perspective.

I've been told of an entrepreneurship game where students are given a blue button and are asked to trade it over the course of a week, and to bring back the item they had finally traded it for. One story I heard was that of a student who brought back £5,000. It seems that the student just went to look for the context where every item was most urgently needed, and the button was traded for a safety pin, which in turn was traded for an expensive pen, and it goes on. £5,000 for a button? No, £5,000 for a series of trades in context.

What this means is that when we buy out of context rather than closer-to-use context, the need for the offering is often seriously discounted to the extent that willingness to pay could be low. I am not proposing that firms exploit context pricing but that customers may prefer to *have a choice* of buying at diminished prices (out of context) as well as buying at a higher price (in context). Economists call this 'mixed bundling' (Venkatesh & Mahajan, 1993), a pricing practice which has been proven to improve revenues for firms. We see this with contract (pay monthly) and pay-as-you-go (prepaid) telco services, but of course most telcos will make you choose one or the other. Somehow, I don't think they quite get it.

The long and short of it is that for all the choices of products in the world, they are mostly out-of-context choices. Today's firms are not very creative in offering contextual choices. This will change with digital technology and competition. Already, supermarkets are starting to understand the market advantage they get from serving contexts (see the case study below on how grocery shopping becomes part of the context of shoppers' daily commute).

There are two further reasons to focus on experience or use contexts:

**Profiling contexts means better targeting of customers**. By focusing on contexts, we can focus on *contextual archetypes* – clusters of social contexts that are similar. The way I make tea may be a contextual archetype that is shared with others who make tea around the same time and place. The focus is on the activities surrounding the making of tea, rather than on just who I am. In the past, when the focus was on exchange value, much attention was given to individuals' choices. So who I am and whether I am the Earl Grey or green tea type of tea buyer was important. As a result, individuals are profiled according to their characteristics so that we can understand the relationship between choice and the individual.

---

## CASE STUDY: The future of grocery shopping – the virtual supermarket

You're returning from your holiday to an empty fridge, and you have guests arriving the next day who need to be fed. What do you do?

Upon arrival at the airport, you find a virtual grocery store where you can browse through images of grocery items on lighted billboards. You select your item, then use your smartphone to scan its barcode or QR code to add the item to your online basket. You pay for your shopping online, then arrange to have it delivered to your home just in time to cook a meal for your guests.

Welcome to the future of grocery shopping. This trial interactive grocery store was introduced by British grocer Tesco at London's Gatwick airport, following the success of Tesco Homeplus's first virtual store in the subway in Seoul, South Korea.

In a bid to take on local competitor e-Mart, Tesco decided to 'let the store come to the people' by creating virtual stores that would become part of people's daily commute. The virtual stores at subways and bus stops not only turned busy commuters' waiting time into shopping

> **(cont.)**
>
> time, but also saved them a trip to the local supermarket on the weekend, hence freeing up more of their leisure time for other pursuits. Since April 2011, Tesco Homeplus's Smartphone App has become the number one shopping app in Korea, with over 900,000 downloads.
>
> Inspired by Tesco's success in South Korea, online health and beauty retailer Well.ca introduced Canada's first-ever virtual store at a busy subway station in downtown Toronto in early 2012. There were more than a hundred app downloads in the first three hours after it rolled out the virtual store.
>
> The success of these innovations hinges on consumer convenience and competence.

However, when we focus on value-in-context, we need to shift our attention away from the individual, to what Normann (2001) would call *activity sets*; i.e., the context of the experience. Instead of profiling individuals, we should be profiling contexts. This is so that we can understand which contexts enable value creation, and how.

What does a context profile mean exactly? Well, think about the use of your music player or even your mug. What is the most frequent context in which you use them? I would say many would use the music player to listen to music when they are on a train, a bus or a plane. Many others would consider having a cup of coffee in the morning is when they use their mugs. It is therefore not surprising that many people share the same context when using a mug or a music player, and it is likely that their activities are similar.

This is not just because music players or mugs are similar but because of what we call *isomorphism*, which is when we start to mimic what others do and end up behaving very similarly to one another in such contexts. This results in contextual archetypes that are similar even among different people. Understanding contexts means understanding patterns of an environment and activities that surround the object and the service it renders, i.e., the *value-creating service system*, because these are the activities within the system that create value of the object in context.

**Redesigning contexts**. Since context is where value creation happens, we can now try to understand the way interactions happen *and how they could change* with different products and technology. Only by focusing on context can we begin to understand how to design future products and technologies to play a role in value creation, and how new offerings could serve contexts better, resulting in new markets.

The widespread adoption of smartphones, satnavs, mobile computing and the millions of sensors and chips that fuel the 'IoT' enables a greater connectivity where all human-made objects can provide information on their location and physical properties. This provides huge opportunities for multiple organisations to connect and collaborate in unique ways to meet customers' needs at specific times and locations.

For example, parcel delivery companies are using customer location data to link up with petrol stations, gyms and even pubs to deliver parcels to people on the way to/from work. Train manufacturers and operators have recognised that the train is the enabler for the outcome of getting to the destination. Dynamic information on identifying an appropriate train, booking tickets, how the train is running, how to get to the station, how to get heavy luggage onto the train, where to sit or whether connecting services are running to schedule: all of this connected and digitised information is creating new markets for companies because they are potential services rendered to us in context.

To understand how future offerings could serve contexts better, we need to understand and describe contexts in a generic way.

CHAPTER 3 REFLECTIONS

We started this chapter by considering how the individual consumer plays a huge role in creating the outcomes that make a purchase worthwhile – but, of course, these experiences can only occur *after* that purchase.

One of the many reasons why 'goods-dominant logic' reigned supreme was the quite scary thought that if value was not fixed but subject to the variability of every customer's context – a unique set of influences and circumstances – we would end up with an almost infinite range of pricing possibilities.

We are, however, not so very individualistic as might be imagined, and it is possible not only to identify the 'invariances' in our 'herd-like' behaviour patterns but also for firms to use these insights around 'activity sets' for better targeting.

It is not difficult to understand that digital offerings – with fingers on buttons but heads in (networked) clouds – can voluntarily (or not) provide vast quantities of data revealing much more of the usage contexts.

For the designer, this digital capacity for better targeting provides a new focus on value creation and for the investor and producer, the economies of scale needed to create new markets. As never before, commercial success now depends on customer competence (their skills) and their perceptions of convenience.

We need therefore a better understanding of the 'contextual experiences'. In the next chapter, we will consider the impacts of our new-found capacity for a more holistic 'whole systems' approach to design for better customer experiences in a world where the responsibilities of the producer no longer terminate 'in a tin'.

# 4   Lifting the lid off context – the contextual experience

There is no doubt whatever about the influence of architecture
and structure upon human character and action. We make
our buildings and afterwards they make us. They regulate the course
of our lives.

Winston Churchill, addressing the English Architectural Association, 1924

Shifting our focus on value to the creation of something good with
offerings within a context is not an easy task. We have spent years
thinking of value as economic exchange; it is very difficult to change
this mindset, regardless of how compelling the argument. In this new
world of value-in-use created in context (i.e., value-in-context),
we have very few frameworks. How can we start thinking about
value creation in context? Is the notion just too fuzzy and vague?
Is value-in-context beyond the reach of systematic analysis?

**Rethinking service**. Fortunately, scholars in the service research
domain have made several advances in this area. Some of us recognise
that inanimate objects, particularly digitised offerings, could offer
resources to achieve some competencies to individuals within a
context – i.e., provide a service within a system (Spohrer et al.,
2007). The service-dominant (S-D) logic (Vargo & Lusch, 2004; 2008)
for value creation implies that when things and people come together
to create value, they come together as a holistic system which we
can view from sociological, anthropological, marketing, business,
engineering and technological perspectives.

I define service as *a competency to create value*, and a service
system as a contextual configuration of entities that render competencies to create systemic outcomes using their competencies (i.e., their
service) in context. As an example, think about a man and woman

having breakfast together. There are many entities in the system. Coffee, tea, bacon, sausages, cups, forks, table, etc. Typically, the system can be described from three perspectives: by the man, the woman, or someone outside looking at them having breakfast.

In truth, there are actually many other perspectives if you take the perspective of every object in context. These perspectives are important because each object is a value proposition from a particular 'vertical' industry; e.g., the cup belonging to the household items industry and therefore representing their value propositions in context. If you are describing the service system from the perspective of the value of the cup, then it must be the service system of the cup and its interactions with the value creator as well as other objects and people within a context.

Yet to understand life contexts as service systems, the science is divided (Ng et al., 2011). There are two different perspectives taken when we look at service systems. The first is reductionism which is widely adopted. This is the way most of us have been taught. If your monitor is faulty, unplug it and get it repaired. Plug it in after repair and everything should work fine. Similarly, if your roof has a problem, we fix the roof and all is well.

But not all systems work like this. When objects and people are more tightly coupled, you can't just reduce it to the component parts. For example, if you have a pain in your elbow, you may not realise that it could be because the chair you are sitting on is too high/low, resulting in the elbow paying the price for poor posture. The chair is external to the whole, and reducing the whole to its component parts and optimising an internal component will not provide relief from the pain.

The more interactive, holistic approach is called systems thinking, which is used much less frequently but has the potential to offer a different set of insights when we think about value-creating contexts. In no sense are these two approaches in competition. Rather, they are complementary, and both provide insights into life phenomena. The box on p. 45 explains the difference between reductionism and systems thinking.

## Reductionism and systems thinking

**Reductionism**. Science is based around the 3Rs of reduction, repeatability and refutation. That is, we *reduce* the world through the selection of variables we can test, and then we run *repeated* experiments until exceptions occur either to *refute* or uphold our original hypotheses.

- Much scientific thinking throughout history is reductionist because many problems are complex and messy. It is easier to focus efforts and select some aspects of a problem from all those that are possible for more detailed study. Basically, reduction of a large challenging problem to the bits you think you can solve is managerially attractive.
- Science progresses by applying the principle of Occams razor: the removal of all extraneous factors to see if you can find a simpler explanation of the facts.
- Science follows Descartes's advice to analyse problems piecemeal, that is, by breaking down a phenomena into its elemental parts.

This approach to scientific thinking strongly influences the manner in which many business academics approach their research. Yet we would argue that the reductionist approach is based on a number of assumptions that we should consider before applying it to other problems, especially in understanding value and contexts.

The first and most crucial assumption, the division of the complex problem into separate parts, means the elements of the whole are the same when examined independently *of* the whole, as when they are examined *as* a whole. Think about it. If the elements are loosely connected, then we can take them apart, analyse them, improve or change them and put them back together, and the whole will be improved. This might be possible with problems of physics at the atomic level, but would it hold for complex wholes? For example, can we take out a part of the body such as the heart, modify it and replace it within the body and not expect wider impacts?

The parts of the whole in the system are not merely interconnected. Their relationships and interoperabilities are also highly complex and

**(*cont.*)**

non-linear. Thus, if we want to understand how a context enables the value creation of a cup, but we have begun the understanding by following a method of reduction (e.g., just looking at the interaction between the value creator and the cup, and not others in the same context), we are making three highly questionable assumptions:

- the connections between the elements (extending the breakfast example above: cup, bacon, newspaper) must be very weak;
- the relationship between the elements must be linear so that the parts can be summed together to make the whole; and
- optimising each part will optimise the whole.

Clearly, many systems do not exhibit those assumptions, so we require an approach that begins with the whole and concentrates on the relationship of the parts in the whole. This is the perspective taken by systems thinkers.

**Systems thinking**. Systems thinking would consider every element in a system as having a role in the whole as well as being a part, but the property of the whole does not exist in the elemental part.

First, this means the elements are interdependent, i.e., they affect one another, and systems thinking is particularly associated with the study of elements that have strong connections, as problems with weak connections are amenable to reduction. Second, there is the notion of the study of 'wholes'. And third, there is the idea that there are properties which occur in the whole that do not occur in the component parts, which is of course the essence of the famous phrase attributed to Aristotle, that 'the whole is greater than the sum of its parts'.

In short, systems thinking is concerned with the study of wholes that exhibit strong interconnections, and as a result of these interconnections, properties emerge at the level of the whole that are not present in the elements.

**Emergence.** Of central importance to seeing the world from a systems perspective is this concept of emergence – probably the most important and challenging idea in systems thinking. Understanding

**(cont.)**

emergence sheds light on what appears as a paradox; that the whole is made up of a set of elements, yet the whole is also different from the elemental parts.

Take for example the harmony of a group of musicians. The property 'harmony' is not found in the component parts (say, the vocalist and guitar) but only occurs when they interact with one another. Other frequently used examples include colour (a phenomenon that can only occur because of the arrangement of the constituent parts in an atom), the swarming of bees, hurricanes, traffic jams and many would argue, life itself.

A fundamental principle is that emergent properties are essentially unpredictable; indeed, one well-used definition of emergence is that it cannot be predicted (otherwise it would be deterministic) but is 'subjectively surprising'. Henle argues that 'where there is an emergent there is unpredictability and that we have emergence where a new form appears and where the causes of the appearance are unable to explain the form' (Henle, 1942).

This does not mean that everything that is unpredictable is emergent, for it may mean we have not as yet developed the model that explains the underlying relationships. The argument here is that given a known starting position and knowledge of the components of the system, we may not know what the outcome of the system could be.

There are many contexts we can analyse which sit at a 'higher' level; e.g., interactions between institutions and people in a network such as a village or community. Context therefore sits in various layers and levels of aggregation (Chandler & Vargo, 2011). However, the focus of this book is on the creation of new markets, so I focus on the lowest (micro) layer of context, which is the value-creating activity set of an individual.

So what are these contexts? If you look at how individuals live their lives, we are more similar than we think. To have an idea of what context is, we have to think about an object, say a TV or a kettle.

Then think about how this object participates in many scenarios – how many contexts a kettle serves. So the kettle could serve the function of 'making tea or coffee', 'when you want hot water for cooking (instead of waiting for water to boil on a stove)' or 'providing hot water to warm plates or sterilise a needle'.

The contextual experiences of an individual around the items acquired consist of five components that need to be understood:

(1) the scope of the context as a system (the perspective and boundaries);
(2) the elements of the context with their *affordances* (value propositions);
(3) the systemic (practices) and structural (rules) of context (value creation);
(4) the individual in context (the value creator) and the *agency*;
(5) the emergent outcomes from value created in context (outcomes).

I will first describe each one, then go on to explain the connections between them.

## THE SCOPE OF THE CONTEXT AS A SYSTEM

The first step towards understanding value-creating context as a service system is to take a stand on what exactly we are looking at, and from whose perspective. This definition of the 'system in focus' means we define where our boundaries are and the scope of what we are looking at. If we do not do that, then a simple context such as 'tea-making' could extend into a huge context that includes where the tea came from, how the kettle was made and how the water got into the house, since each of these extensions has some bearing on the value-creating context. Also, if we don't take on a perspective, everyone in a context has a different description of the system, as I have explained previously.

It is also important that the value creator's level of *comprehension* of the context is taken into account. When an individual interacts with elements in context, his or her knowledge influences the contextual value creation because one could view the system as complex while another would see it as being simple. Tea-making is simple to some people, but complex to a person with dementia. So while we might consider value-creating context to be from the perspective of a notional 'ordinary person', we must recognise the level of complexity of the context as part of the scope of the system. This is particularly important when we begin to think of digital interventions (covered in the second half of this book), where the ability to interact with devices and other objects that lend resources to a system may vary for different individuals with different levels of skills and knowledge. If we wanted to understand the context of a home as different activity sets for different people from the young to the old, we must see their competencies and knowledge as part of – and not separate from – the archetypes.

In addition, it is important to specify whether the perception of the context and its dynamics comes from an observer who is *internal* or *external* to the observed system. Perceiving an event from inside the context is different from observing the event from outside the context. The space-time perspective taken by the observer based on whether or not he or she is the main actor in the system, is a crucial element with respect to the relevant elements in context as well as what interactions matter. In the case of value-creating contexts, an *insider* (value creator) view is essential. Yet, before you start to think that every value creator is different (which of course is true) and therefore not scalable for firms to serve, the value-creating contexts may not

be that different if you consider that the activities and interactions may be similar even for different people. Within a certain culture, there are patterns of similarity in terms of how we unwind after dinner, take the children out to the park or commute to work.

Every value-creating context is a whole system, and within the whole are its entities or elements. To understand the system, we need to understand the connections that result in the 'whole' system. The notion of 'wholeness', i.e., for all elements to 'behave' appropriately within the value creation context, must mean that the whole is composed in a certain way, and this composition is the initial mapping to define the scope of the system in focus. It is this wholeness that provides the basis for contextual archetypes across people.

## THE ELEMENTS IN CONTEXT

The elements are the persons, places, things and conditions; what we can think of as *nouns*. As an example, let's say I am having tea with a friend in my garden. The elemental context would be the cups, saucers, plates, tea, pot, cake, chair, table, decking, umbrella, sunshine, garden and the person with whom I am having tea. These are all items that could be naturally provided (e.g., sunshine) or acquired beforehand (e.g., cups and cakes), but they become the elemental context because I brought them into context.

So I set the scene for all the elements to play a role in context because each one of these elements provide a resource that I can integrate to co-create the value of every item I have purchased, to achieve the outcome of 'tea in the garden'. As mentioned above, some of these elements are naturally occurring (e.g., sunshine), a public good (e.g., a park) or have been manufactured beforehand so that you can realise its value-in-context. Manufactured objects can therefore be considered as 'temporal vessels' of resources to be realised by the individual in use. As a temporal vessel of resources, it could hold potential meaning, and even potential symbolic resources.

Yet, these elements are not just randomly present. They are brought together because we know that these elements can do certain things, and that as individuals, we design the context of value creation according to how these elements can *be performed on*. Gibson (1982) described this as 'affordance'.

Affordance is the quality of something that allows an actor to perform an action upon it. It is an enabling quality. Gibson used linguistic constructs to refer to affordances as '(verb phrase)-able'. For example, an apple is 'eat-able', a stone is 'throw-able', fire is 'cook-with-able'. Gibson considers that the meaning or value of something 'consists of what it affords'. The elements *within a context* therefore depend not merely on the elements, but also on what they afford to create value. So a chair is 'sit-able', tea is 'drink-able', and the elements become resources by which value can be created through their affordances.

Of course, affordance is just a potential of the object. For value to be created, the potential has to be realised and acted upon. Hence, a chair could be 'sit-able' but it is the sitting, the act of the individual, that creates that value. Affordances may be symbolic as well (Pickering, 2007). So if the individual is out to show off to friends, a silver teapot affords 'posh-ambience-creating-able'. So elements can be 'signs' or symbols for affording the creation of meaning for individuals.

However, elements may not always exhibit the same affordances and indeed, may create negative affordances. For example, sunshine may afford 'warmth-creating-able' but it also is 'perspiration-creating-able'. A large umbrella is used to reduce the potential negative affordance and the

umbrella therefore has a positive affordance of 'shade-creating-able'. All this means that elements are only potential resources to create value, and they become resources only in context through a positive affordance acted upon by the individual in a way that creates value.

One way of thinking about elements in context is to consider that all elements have a duality in role. They have a *distinctive* role and a *connective* role.

In its *distinctive* role, any element has characteristics or attributes that are non-contextually driven. These are what firms would call product attributes or features. In the traditional way of thinking, 'customers will gain X benefit due to Z attribute'; e.g., 'customers will gain a stronger immune system from all-in-one multivitamins'.

Of course, this simplistic way of thinking completely negates the role of the customer context in creating that value – they would need to supplement the multivitamins with the right diet, and make sure they take them daily. It is assumed that the benefit is somehow automatically achieved because of the product attribute, and the presumed behaviour or intellect of the customers is rarely acknowledged. Size and colour are typical product attributes for mobile phones; power, spaciousness and safety for cars. The distinctive role, to use the energy analogy, is the product as a *potential* to create value.

The element's affordance is its *connective* role, which is completely driven by the context in which value is created with its experience. So the affordance of a car is 'smooth-drive-ability', which, from its language, would require other elements (weather, traffic) to create value of the car within the system for the outcome (smooth drive home). The connective role is what makes the potential of the product create value 'kinetically'.

The *distinctive* role (product attributes) is the part element of the system that can be disconnected from the system (potential), and the *connective* role is the part-whole of the element where its role contributes to the whole value-creating system through its *affordance* (within the kinetic). Clearly, complexity comes from both the distinctiveness of the elements as well as their connections. As things become more connected, the need to analyse context moves towards the elements' affordance, i.e., the elements' connective, part-whole and kinetic roles within the value-creating system.

## THE STRUCTURAL AND SYSTEMIC CONTEXT

The act of interacting with an object to create value is the socio-material *practice* of the object (Orlikowski, 2007). This is the *systemic* context. It is the context of interactions and practices, i.e., what people DO – which of course, also includes what they say. Meaning is formed by doing, so the act of drinking wine is a meaningful practice of creating value with the wine and the glass. Practices are what make contexts systemic and dynamic; this draws from practice theory, a type of social theory taken from authors such as Bourdieu, Giddens, Taylor, Foucault and other scholars.

Systemic contexts are the 'flows', the 'movement', and what makes a context dynamic and kinetic. They are where actual interactions happen. You can think of them as the *verbs* – *they* are what creates value within a context between the individual and an object, assuming the object is able to afford (enable) that action. We can think of these verbs as the act of consummation between the object's affordance created by the firm who made the object, and the individual value creator acting upon the object – the co-creation of value.

For instance, an individual using a coffee maker does so through many actions – place cup, put coffee beans/powder/capsules into machine, press button, wait, remove cup. The machine must be designed in such a way that *affords* the making of a cup of coffee. The act of making that cup of coffee must still be performed by the individual. Yet, the machine must do the tasks that the individual cannot do, e.g., grind the beans, and create a pressurised environment for water to be mixed with the powder to ensure that a cup of coffee can be produced.

Many individuals may wish their coffee to have milk but the machine can only enable generic coffee-making, and cannot necessarily make the perfect cup of coffee to suit every individual's customised taste. The individual must then integrate his actions with other verb-interactions – get cold milk from the fridge, warm it up, get sugar from the cabinet. The individual is therefore the system integrator, and each object and its affordances enable the person to create the perfect cup of coffee.

The understanding of such ancillary interactions and objects is central in identifying and describing value-creating practices and how they might change with technological interventions. Through the understanding of such interactions and practices, we understand that value created with the object, such as a coffee maker, is not just about how good it is in enabling our actions on the machine. It is also about the ritualistic act of making coffee, which holds meaning for us socially and culturally. Moreover, the negotiation of meanings is not only through the interactions of human actors but also between human actors and objects. Schatzki (1996: p. 89) proposes practice as a 'temporally unfolding and spatially dispersed nexus of doings and sayings'. Value is created through actions or 'verbs' with others, and through enacting the affordance (verb-ability) of the offering in context.

It is important to note that practices of human-to-human systems are not processes. 'Process' suggests some sort of sequentiality that could be mapped in some way, while 'practices' arise from the interdependency between individuals. So you may be able to map the process of making tea for example, but not the practice of a conversation because what one person says will depend on how the other person responds.

Practices of individuals and collective actors can not only reproduce but also transform social conditions under which they act (Giddens, 1984). Indeed, this change might be enabled and enhanced by our adoption of technologies. Before the advent of social networks, 'family' was a social construction that required physical presence of people. Today, family and communities can be socially and virtually constructed with reduced physical interactions. Technology has afforded the communication between family members across the world through Skype and Facetime, but human agents must feel that they are able to create value freely with the technologies and interact among themselves for these virtual constructions to be realised.

The structural context refers to 'rules' or 'norms' within the social context of value creation. Rules become *norms* that bind us and create traditions that are enduring. Social norms and rules govern our behaviours, and are the reasons why we may have wine with our dinner in some cultures, but not in others.

Rules and norms are embedded in all actions, from the simple act of whether milk is added before or after we pour hot water over the teabag, to how we bring up our children. Even the manner through which we interact with objects, such as when we watch TV or the kind of DIY activities we choose to take up, is a part of the norms we live with. They also exist in the practices we take for granted in our day-to-day life, e.g., how we greet people, or how we use everyday objects. Norms, once established, become embedded in the way we achieve outcomes. More importantly, norms are passed down and practices that are the norm become consistently the same over time.

The structural context for creating value is therefore governed by the normative rules that dictate the manner in which we interact and make things happen. The structural and systemic contexts are inseparable from each other. Yet, the norms and practices are not 'out there' as though they are external to us. Rather, they are part of us, and in the way we interact with others and with objects (verbs). We create the rules as well as reinforce them; this is what Giddens refers to as duality.

Structures both aid and impede us in our actions. For example, if someone asked you to walk across a large field but you find no path at all, you may be reluctant to walk across it. Yet, if someone told you that there was a path but it seems to be a longer route, you may be tempted to walk on the field where there is no path.

Normative rules are a bit like that path. Often, we take it without thinking why we do what we do, but sometimes it also impedes what we do without us even being aware of it. Other times, we may think about how we might do things differently but these normative rules exist to comply with and contest against our behaviour. Without them, we may not even be willing to act. This is why these social norms are referred to as structures. They are analogical to the physical structures around us that implicitly govern where and how we move.

Structure dictates the type of connections between the elements of the whole – the way the system is internally organised. Behaviour of elements amid individuals emerge from structure. Structural context is a static representation of context while systemic context consists of its dynamic 'flows'. In natural systems, structure means the laws of nature while system is the sequence, process and rhythm of the activities of the entities. In social systems such as a weekend at home, structure is the static description of roles, activities and tasks performed in compliance with rules and constraints, and system is the dynamic movement of activities and actions resulting in the flow of actions and information between entities.

In such social systems, a structure can be studied objectively (What is it? How is it made?) while a system can only be interpreted (How does it work? What logic does it follow?). This means that from a static structure, the dynamic interpretation of reality suggests recognition of various possible systems that are dependent on the outcomes that the entities wish to achieve.

This is an essential methodological step forward in the investigation of value-creating contexts. It introduces a relevant distinction between a perspective based on the observation of elements and features characterising the structure of the observed phenomenon (structure representation), and a perspective based on the interpretation of its dynamics (systems representation). The key to complexity is not to think of a system as 'complex', but to consider that complexity as being embedded in decisions and actions. If we didn't need to decide or act, it wouldn't be complex (Badinelli et al., 2012). If we do, then the system is bounded by the perspective of the person who has to act or decide and the context of those decisions and actions; it is not as though the system is complex by itself.

The structural and systemic contexts also govern communication and indeed, the type of information that is needed and communicated. As social individuals, we learn when and where it is appropriate to say certain things. We are often careful with our choice of words, and mindful of when it is suitable to discuss certain topics or wear some types of clothes, and also when it is not. These social and cultural norms regulate our behaviours as well as our need for information, and we come to know this often through our consumption experience (Hirshman & Holbrook, 1982); we learn them through interactions.

The structural context plays an important role in our need for information and in turn, shapes our demand for information embedded in new digital products and offerings that could better serve contexts.

## THE INDIVIDUAL IN CONTEXT

**Context practices**. To create value, individuals must have the skills and competencies to act in context so that outcomes can be achieved. These skills and competencies translate into resources in context to create value, and the individual enacts the practices to transform his or her skills into resources to achieve outcomes. Being able to drink beer when the football game is on, is a practice that requires skill and competencies – try telling that to your male colleagues. In the case of making the cup of coffee, individuals must believe that they have the skill to do so. Hence, if you consider that the *practice* of making a cup of coffee is the way you create value with a coffee maker, you must also consider a further point – that of human *agency*.

Agency is the capacity of an individual to act independently and to make their own free choices (Barker, 2000). We have seen that structure refers to institutionalised 'norms or patterns' that may enable or disable choices and opportunities. Agency, on the other hand, is the ability of an individual to act in spite of, or because of, the structure. Structure and agency are big topics in sociology and cultural studies. In a way, agency is the mirror concept to affordance. The way an object is designed and manufactured as a *potential* to afford value creation in a *kinetic* way is mirrored through the way I consider individuals as having skills and competencies as potential, so that they have the agency to experience or use the object in a *kinetic* way to create that value.

Agency means the person has to apply some sort of judgement where the act is an endorsement that they have accepted the consequence of an action. For example, there are many cases in social situations where it may be inappropriate for certain persons to act in a certain way, even if the outcomes may be beneficial. You may be very hungry going into a dinner party, but you may not take out the apple in your pocket because it is inappropriate to do so. In this case,

you do not have agency within that context to create value with that apple. Similarly, the challenges of many new technologies come from the fact that many who are unfamiliar with them may not consider themselves to have agency to use a device, due to fear of technology or other reasons.

To create phenomenological value, individuals assert their active agency to transform offerings and value propositions to achieve their consumers' self, life project and goals (Arnould, 2005; 2007; Cova & Dalli, 2009). Current marketing literature on consumer culture theory (CCT) describes consumer agency as one's ability to engage fully in all of the various aspects of consumption. It is through the consumer's ability to act within a context to create value that affordances of offerings could be enacted and outcomes achieved (McCracken, 1986; Arnould & Thompson, 2005; Shankar et al., 2006). Such an agency may be constrained in context (e.g., there is no light to do work, or the boss is around so you can't get on Facebook), and the value of that offering may then not be created as a consequence.

## THE EMERGENT OUTCOMES FROM VALUE CO-CREATION IN CONTEXT

The value we create with each of the offerings we have acquired is the goodness that results from our interactions with these offerings. As such, each offering is a value proposition for us to realise and create value-in-context. The interactions are not linear, nor are they transactional. They are systemic and kinetic, with the value created arising from the interactions with each one of them.

However, each offering does not exist in isolation. We create value from bread but this is usually because we are also creating value with butter and jam, juice and cereal as the different elements in context of having breakfast. It is the creation of phenomenological value through practices in the social contextual system that results in emergent outcomes, such as a good and nutritious breakfast (Bourdieu, 1977; Reckwitz, 2002; Warde, 2005). The contextual system, where collective value is created with different offerings, becomes better off and the entire system, as defined by the value creator, becomes more viable (Vargo et al., 2008) because the value (co-)creator is able to make the whole better than the sum of its parts.

This is therefore the phenomenon of lived experience. It is how individuals interact with products as we use them, i.e., the actual engagement and use experience of the offerings, through which we create meaning in our lives (Holbrook, 2006).

The elements are the *value propositions* (*potential*) necessary for the practices of value creation, while the individual in context brings skills and competencies, i.e., their value propositions to enact the practices. The structural context 'sets the scene' for value creation; it creates the *medium* for behaviours but the actual value creation occurs within the *practices* of the systemic context, which is *how* the value is actually *created*.

Yet, these practices can only happen if each offering has the necessary affordance, the individual has the necessary agency, and the context is set such that all elements that are necessary are available in context. So the cup and the saucer may be the resource proposition of a posh china company to afford tea-drinkability and posh-creating-ability but the individual must know the skill of conduct to act on the china, and the tea set must have been laid out for use beforehand. Within the context of a garden party, what is considered to be the norm of having tea in the garden will, to some extent, regulate the actual behaviour, and the individual will enact those behaviours, aided by the affordance of the offerings to create the phenomenological value of the tea set.

Clearly, as all five components of contexts are social constructions (even the perception of the material element, especially in terms of the potential meaning or action it affords), there is a dynamic interplay between them. For example, contexts could lend further resources to individuals or the offering's affordance could interact with the actor's agency. The context or system where the value is created collectively becomes better off because, as I mentioned before, the value creator is able to make the interactions between the different offerings work well to create that whole that is better than the sum of its parts (see Figure 4.1).

The diagram of my integrated framework of value (Ng & Smith, 2012) proposes the relationship between the social and the material through a 'relational ontology', which privileges neither humans nor

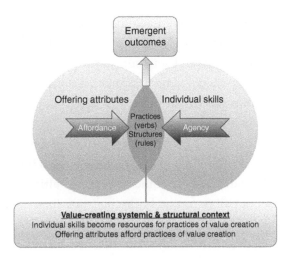

FIGURE 4.1: Integrated framework of value

objects, nor treats humans and things as separate and different realities, an ontology suggested by Orlikowski (2009). However, it also emphasises the inseparable relationship between the social and the material (Orlikowski, 2007). It is also important to stress that the five elements are not distinct or hierarchical in any sense. They merely illustrate the concept of possible archetypes of value-creating contexts. Getting these archetypes of contexts right would help firms design scalable offerings of the future.

To take another example, city authorities may desire to invest in a vastly better digital network infrastructure, with the intended outcome of a revitalised local economy. The outcome will however only be realised if the network offering has the necessary affordance, and within the community there is the necessary agency set in contexts of a series of programmes to deliver skills, inclusion, information access, innovation development and location-marketing. The initial investment does not magically produce the desired outcome by itself.

While I say that the nouns and rules enable value creation, they could also easily disable value creation. Poorly designed products that do not consider the systems they are used within are examples of how value creation could be impeded. For example, you may have window blinds that separate from the centre, while the window opens on the right. Therefore, when you have the window open, the blinds flap in the wind and make a noise. Had the blinds been separated from the right to left, you could move the blinds to open *with* the window.

Value creation could also be impeded when products do not comply with social rules. An app that talks and pokes fun at different accents may be offensive to some groups, resulting in negative outcomes. Also, not all norms and rules play out differently in different environments. You might listen to your mp3 player while on the bus, but not during a meeting with the boss. The environment for such norms may also not just be physical. For example, it may be acceptable to take photos in a church for a wedding but not in the same church during a funeral.

Once we understand this, we begin to see why context should be the focus for the future. This is an important change in mindset. Previously we considered the value of an offering as the essence of an object. With this shift in mindset, we can now consider value as the goodness arising from the experience of the object and by logical extension, we have to consider that experience to be part of

a system of objects and people in creating value. So objects are not seen as having 'intrinsic' value, but are 'positional' within a context. This is why value-in-use/experience is often referred to as value-in-context. It is the creation of value-in-context that leads us to the outcomes we want (whether emotional or functional).

There are reasons why I have delved so deeply into value creation and analysed it in a systematic way:

- First, creating new markets from digitally connected offerings means we must be able to think about how to influence or *intervene* in value-creating systems in new and effective ways, *because digitally connected offerings are able to do so.*
- Second, the future of markets depends on how firms can charge in different ways that are not merely about exchanging goods and services. Understanding value creation in context brings forward different *revenue or economic models* and commercial viability for future offerings.
- Finally, understanding value creation in context helps us think about the *design* of future offerings for their use and experience, rather than just exchange.

All this will be covered further along the book but first, there is a need to understand how value created with an object is linked to exchange. Without understanding how consumers buy and how firms could profit from participating in value-creating systems, firms will not even create the value propositions in the first place.

CHAPTER 4 REFLECTIONS

A traditional approach to problem-solving is to take the thing apart, look at the components, fix them, reassemble and then retest them. This simple and straightforward approach is easily managed, but it is not appropriate when the parts are interdependent with one another, and an issue in one place may have repercussions in another.

Reductionism – reducing things to a component level – doesn't always fit when, by virtue of the complex interconnectedness of an entire system, we sense that 'the whole is greater than the sum of its parts'. An appreciation of the need for systems thinking has been on the rise for decades. You may recall the reference at the start of Chapter 1 where Arno Penzias described this more harmonious era of intense interoperability – 'making things that work with other things'.

The need to understand this more holistic approach leads us to consider usage contexts as a system – a connective complex that includes the skill and actions of the user and their normal rules of behaviour. Describing the distinction between a 'structural context' – how the system is made up – and a 'systemic context' – the inter-actions of value creation – is also impacted by our perspective. Are we looking in as an outsider, or are we looking out from a user perspective, or even from an object-in-context perspective? Perspective must be embedded whenever we talk about a system. Often, policy-makers or top-down management talk about systems as though they are 'out there', and we all see the same system when in actual fact, the system of a room depends on which part of the room you are standing and the decisions and actions you need to make about the room.

This chapter has explored the process of value creation in a very detailed way because 'whole systems thinking' represents the challenges and opportunities afforded by new flexibilities from digitisation. In the next chapter – Value and exchange – we consider how this might align with wealth creation.

# 5    Value and exchange

PLATO'S ALLEGORY OF THE CAVE

*The allegory of the cave (also known as an analogy of the cave) was used by the Greek philosopher Plato in his work* The Republic *to highlight the nature and need for education. It was written as a dialogue narrated by Plato's friend Socrates and Plato's brother Glaucon.*

*Socrates describes a group of prisoners who have lived chained to the wall of a cave all of their lives while facing a blank wall. The prisoners see shadows projected on the wall of things passing in front of a fire situated behind them, and they begin to describe these shadows as their reality, giving the shadows form and terms. Socrates explains that the shadows are as close as the prisoners will ever get to viewing reality, and in fact, the shadows* are *their reality. He then explains how the philosopher is like a freed prisoner from the cave*

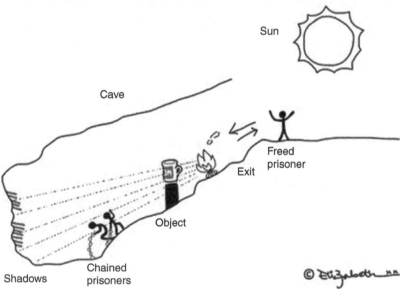

Sun

Cave

Freed prisoner

Exit

Object

Shadows

Chained prisoners

© Elizabeth

*who realises that the shadows on the wall are not reality after all, as*
*he can perceive another form of reality. Socrates considers this a*
*'true' form of reality, although modern philosophers may consider*
*that this is just another form of reality. However, this other form of*
*reality enlightens the freed prisoner as he can see why and how the*
*shadows could exist, and understand how the prisoners still chained*
*to the wall would perceive the shadows as their reality.*

This chapter starts with the allegory of the cave to convey an
important point on value. I want to use it to emphasise what I had
discussed in Chapter 2; how the world as we know it has reduced the
concept of value to that of *worth*.

Worth, then, is the shadow reality of value. True value is the
goodness created from our experience and interactions with objects
and other people. Worth, as a measure of that goodness, is a shadow,
but one that has been given form, language and structure, and we have
been made to believe that it is the reality. I propose that it is not. This
belief is however not entirely false either; as a shadow it is some
vision of reality, but it is a shadow nonetheless.

Worth is a shadow of reality because it is created out of the need
to form exchanges. As I explained in Chapter 2, a market economy
that relies on market forces to allocate goods and resources and to
determine prices for them requires us to think about exchanges as
involving some form of compensation for both parties to achieve each
party's outcomes. The need for compensation so that an exchange can
happen requires a way to assess the worth of an offering and a way of
paying for it. Modern market economies have efficient institutions
and channels for assessing objects and creating ways to pay for them.
Today, you can buy online, on mobile, at a shop, through agents,
catalogues and even in social settings of Tupperware parties.

Since there must be compensation to both parties for exchange to
occur, each party must assess the worth of what is being exchanged. For
the customers, our assessment of worth is in terms of the value created
upon acquiring the offering, while for the firm, they must assess the
cost of creating that worth and engaging in that value creation in

context. Economists consider these assessments as 'transaction costs', which determine the viable options for firms to sell to customers as well as the viable options for customers to buy. For customers and firms to be able to come together to exchange through whatever channel means that, using the language of economists, the market is able to 'clear' and there is a market price mechanism to compensate all parties. This is an important point to note as the channels for exchange and interaction are changing and in some cases (most evident on the Facebook platform) there may not be a market price mechanism. This will be covered in the last two chapters of the book.

Viability to create offerings and exchange them in markets is a crucial factor in order to serve our needs. For example, we would love to have milk magically appear at our doorsteps whenever we've run out of it. To achieve this however, the firm must put in place an information system that would alert them whenever we need milk, and arrange to have it sent to us. However, it's probably not viable for the firm to do so, as we will never buy enough milk to justify their installation of a system to serve us individually. Nor is it viable for us if the firm passes on to us the cost of installing that system. It would however probably be viable if both parties met halfway. The firm could send milk to the neighbourhood convenience store, and we would then only need to walk 500 meters to buy it. The firm achieves its viability from the revenues generated due to the many customers who will walk to the store to get their milk (demand), and supplying the store becomes a scalable option as well since increasing demand just means supplying more of the same. This works until a competitor comes in and finds a viable option to serve us all at home at our point of need, which is possible with advancing technologies.

Notice however, that most times, the firm receives its compensation almost upon exchange, i.e., when we pay the money. However, *we* don't get our 'compensation' when we buy. We get it when we use. It is therefore important to understand how the value we create with an offering is related to our assessment of worth. This understanding is critical for the future of new markets and exchanges.

## ASSESSING WORTH

For years, marketing scholars have been teaching MBA students the basics of marketing, but it's important as we move into a technologically advanced age, that we remind ourselves of these fundamental principles. All purchases start from individual needs. From our needs come our desires or wants, which are the ways we would like our needs to be satisfied. So I may be hungry in the morning, which is a need, but I might desire some toast while my daughter would prefer cereal.

When the desire for something is backed by purchasing power, demand for that 'something' emerges and a market for that 'something' develops. Fundamentally, markets are developed around offerings that are solutions to needs that have purchasing power. It is of course easier to understand this when there is already something to look at, an existing object or offering, and we can rationalise how an offering came to have a market for it. For new technologically disruptive products however, it is incredibly hard to see what needs could be fulfilled and how new markets could develop from them.

What marketing books don't often talk about when we buy things is the fact that while the assessment of worth by a customer often occurs at the point of exchange, value creation occurs at the point of experiential use. This is understandable because markets are created at the points of exchange, so the focus has been less about value creation in context but more about where exchanges happen. Yet to progress, we must ask an important question: what is the relationship between value and worth? To understand that, we must understand how we consciously perceive value.

**Consciousness of value**. When we create value-in-context with offerings, i.e., the goodness that we create from experiencing/using these objects, it is created phenomenologically. We don't really think about it; we just use and experience things, and live our lives the way we want to. This means that value creation happens as a raw experience out of movement, forms, sounds, sensations, emotions and feeling. Block (1977) calls this *phenomenal consciousness*.

So when we bake a cake in the kitchen, the tools and ingredients are what we use and experience, but we don't really think about

the value we are creating;
we are just living our lives.
Similarly, if you are in your
tool shed, the power tools
and the project you are
immersed in are all part of
the contextual experience,
and you don't normally
think about the value of
things.

At the point of
buying, or at the point when
we are asked to assess
the worth of something, we may then become aware of what we
are buying and why we are buying it. This means we have a
more heightened consciousness of the potential value to be created,
which is called *access-consciousness*. Access-consciousness is perception, introspection, reflection; in a sense, a more heightened awareness
of the phenomenon of value creation.

I argue that it is the access-consciousness of value (A-C value)
that leads us to the perception of *worth*, that drives our choices when
we buy something and that influences our evaluation after purchase
and use; whether or not it was good. Worth is therefore an assessment
of the A-C value created.

For simplicity's sake, let's call A-C value *imagined value*, in the
way that results in a decision – whether the imagined value would
make you better off, since you have to spend money to acquire the
offering, as well as design the contextual resources (e.g., effort) in
experiential use contexts. Exchange happens only when you feel you
would be better off. So the money given up to buy something occurs
only when that something has 'value for money', but it is actually a
confirmation that you believe you would be better off if you had
bought it.

I hesitate to call imagined value 'utility' because utility suggests imagined value to be some sort of essence within a thing, when

imagined value is actually our imagined goodness arising from the *system* of value creation subconsciously sitting in our heads. So the utility of a drill could be our assessment of the drill's usefulness (its essence), but imagined value is our assessment of the many value-creating systems in which we could experience the drill, which includes the other elements in our possession and the structural and systemic aspects of those systems.

Here's a good way to think about imagined value: you are planning to buy a juicer and just as you are about to pay for it, your significant other tells you that there is no place for it on the kitchen counter. This means that each time you want to use the juicer, you would need to take it out of the kitchen cabinet, clean it after use, then put it back in the cabinet. At that moment, the juicer and its benefits remain the same, but the system of value creation imagined in your head has changed and you may be less willing to buy it. So, reducing imagined value to utility therefore does not quite do it justice. This is important for the future of digital connectivity that allows different kinds of business models to intervene in value-creating systems, both imagined and real.

Whether or not that imagined value perceived by us is the same as the value created, could be re-evaluated differently at different times, since all five elements in creating true phenomenological value could potentially change within the dynamic context of the experience. Worth is often assessed at the point of exchange by the customer, and is subject to the context of purchase at that time. The assessment of worth by a customer, whether it is still the same after the experience, is also based on imagined value, since it's on the same level of consciousness.

Thus, worth is not the enacted phenomenological value gained from the experience of something in the kinetic, but some exchange proxy (usually money) for the imagined value of an offering at the point of exchange. This imagined value is a perception-expectation of the offering (what is it? what could it be?), and its affordance (what does it enable?) within some context (when is it used?) that is acted

upon (what actions?) by
the actor expending its
resources (what is needed?)
to realise that value
phenomenologically.

The worth of an
offering is therefore assessed
in terms of our agency and
the offering's affordance to
achieve the real value
created in the experience
towards our outcomes. The
worth of a burger is high if it
is perceived to be food

(offering), 'eat-able' (affords eating) when 'hungry' (context), you are not
restrained from eating it (agency) and you have the skills and competency
(ability to eat) to do so, and to achieve an outcome (no longer hungry).
Without our perception and belief of the offering's appropriate affordance
and context, or our agency and resources, the burger would be assessed as
not being worth it, as its outcome may not be achieved.

Similarly, a designer handbag could be assessed as high worth if
it is a meaningful brand (offering), 'show-off-able' (affordance) when
'seen in public' (context), when we can carry/experience it (agency)
and match it with the right clothes and be seen in the right places
(skills and competencies), to achieve our outcome (status). The assessment of the worth of an offering is therefore based on an imagined
value to be created with all five components in the experiential
context towards our outcomes. It is the worth of the offering that
informs choice, and repeat purchases would be influenced by the
assessment of worth after the experience.

Extending this, we can now argue for how the *degree* of worth is
assessed. Clearly, worth could be high if the individual perceives the
imagined value created as high. This could occur when there is a
multitude of offerings, affordances (multi-tasking enablement), the
contexts for creating value are many and are highly probable

(e.g., mobile use), and the actor is able to act without constraints (make calls, use data) and have resources (skills).

The worth of an apple is high if the individual has a high probability of creating the imagined value-in-context (e.g., he is hungry right now) and/or the contexts of use are many (he gets hungry very often). Similarly, the eat-ability of an apple is also high if there are multiple affordances within a context (eat-ability and give-to-girlfriend-ability) or if the context is more urgent (he is very hungry).

Therefore, any offering has various degrees of goodness which are uniquely phenomenological when enacted, and which at the point of exchange would influence your willingness to pay and assessment of the worth. After the experience, you would also assess the offering's worth and your level of 'satisfaction', not as a passive evaluator of the offering, but as an assessor of the offering's fit towards your agency and skills and other contextual resources to achieve the outcomes in context.

Such agency and skills could of course be appropriated, obtained or adjusted by the actor to achieve that fit. In other words, post-experience assessment of worth is less about the offering, but more about how an individual chooses to create value around the offering in context and is able to realise that creation.

The concept of worth, as distinct from value, considers value to be phenomenologically determined, that it is 'uniquely and context-ually interpreted' (Vargo & Lusch, 2008). Worth, however, is an assess-ment of imagined value creation and the offering's role within it. This could be assessed before and after the contextual value creation. The money offered to the firm in exchange for the offering is therefore the market economy.

**Paradox of value translated to worth.** Since true value created is within a phenomenon, then phenomenal consciousness value (P-C value) cannot be truly known by nature of its phenomenal conscious-ness, as it sits at a raw experience level. On the other hand, when an individual assesses and becomes conscious of the P-C value, it imme-diately becomes a different consciousness, i.e., it becomes imagined value.

This means that any measurement, assessment, judgement or evaluation of value created, even by the individual himself or herself, can only capture worth based on imagined value, even while true value created is P-C value. Since worth is an assessment of imagined value, there are, of course, grounds to influence worth through promises of what might be actual P-C value, and thus affect the individual's willingness to pay, or assessment of worth. This means that we can never ascertain P-C value. It is this paradox that leads me to conclude that worth is almost always a shadow reality of real phenomenological value.

Worth, however, is an important shadow of value for a few reasons. It is worth that attempts to translate the goodness of value creation into economic measures (e.g., price), so that firms can think about how much they can charge for the role their offerings play in achieving a benefit for the individual. Through that estimation, they can then decide if it is viable to offer the object in the marketplace.

Yet, I propose that while worth is what firms could potentially get in return for the offering, value creation is what the offering has to be designed for. This means that the value a customer creates around the offering is separate but inextricably linked to its worth. From the firm's perspective, value is what they would design an offering for, but worth is what they expect to get in return. As we move on to the next section of the book, this separation becomes more important because very often, the value created around an offering may not be fully able to be captured or internalised by the firm to create worth.

**Temporal discounting**. The difference in the consciousness of value created in context and the individual's assessment (or imagining) of that context contributes to the distortion of worth. This is called *temporal discounting*. Given that worth is assessed at the point of exchange and value is created at the point of experience, we tend to distort the value we create in the past or future because we would be over- or underestimating the value.

Buying an offering outside of context changes the worth when compared to the worth at the point of experiential use; I call this *contextual worth*. Contextual worth is what you would be willing to pay for an offering at the moment when you need it most – which is when you would be creating value with it. Clearly, there is no absolute figure for worth. You could be wanting a bar of chocolate right now and be willing to pay £3 for it, and tomorrow you could also be wanting a bar of chocolate but unwilling to pay this amount for it. Notwithstanding this, buying out of context almost always creates greater uncertainties and temporal distortions, resulting in out-of-context worth to be sometimes higher or lower than contextual worth.

Let us first consider how the imagined value that is created translates to worth of an offering in two temporal ways – in advanced-based and outcome-based exchanges. Each type of exchange to some extent distorts the translation from value to worth, but each has its own peculiarities.

## ADVANCED-BASED EXCHANGES

In advanced-based exchanges, worth is assessed by the customer before use. Objects that we desire to create value with and achieve our outcomes do not suddenly appear in context. As the previous chapter has presented, we design our contexts so that we can create value. If we are going to a party, we might like some nice shoes. Yet, even to design 'going to a party' with some objects (shoes) in mind, means there must be a conscious decision by individuals to acquire these objects. Worth is therefore the assessment by the individual of the value that could be created, if they buy.

The time and space of purchase is what I consider to be the buying context. Clearly, the closer the buying context is to the experiential use context, the closer is the individual's assessment of worth to the potential goodness of the offering (value) achieved through value creation, i.e., the better the person's imagination might be for imagined value. When buying is not at the same time and space of experience though, the individual faces all the contextual and architectural uncertainties that would distort the translation of value to worth. These uncertainties could substantially devalue the potential goodness (value) that could be created with the offering and in turn, reduce its worth.

In normal circumstances, buying in advance of contextual use suffers from five uncertainties:

- **Uncertainty from imagination of benefits/outcomes in use-context**. First, the firm is asking the individual to imagine what the co-creation experience might be like. That's the top uncertainty for the firm in terms of pricing – I call this the uncertainty from a lack of imagination. Herbert Simon (1991) would call it bounded rationality.

  > Example: if you're trying to sell a concert ticket, your customer will not pay if he can't imagine what the concert experience might be. If the individual has experienced a concert previously, he might be able to imagine it better. If not, £100 an hour could now be worth ... maybe £50 due to the lack of imagination?
  >
  > Alternatively, he could have an overactive imagination, thinking that it is worth more, because he has heard so much about the concert. Either way, worth suffers from this uncertainty.

- **Uncertainty of value-creating context**. If this is a repeat purchase, it's a lot easier BUT the context/state of experience might still change. I call this the uncertainty of context.

  > Example: your outdoor concert is perfectly well imagined as customers have attended a similar event previously. However, your repeat customer doesn't think the weather will now be as good. Would a discount of £70 persuade him/her?

We may also not know the rules of a context that may inhibit our actions. So if you have always wanted to go to the theatre but are unsure about dress code or conduct, you may not buy that ticket, or you might consider it as being worth less. Conversely, we might overestimate the contexts for value creation. Buying a tuxedo may seem to be worth it because you overestimate how many times (contexts) you would wear it.

Uncertainty of context is also the uncertainty around the time for value creation. For example, you might think you would only need an hour's worth of parking to get the shopping done but you might take longer, in which case you may have to go back to the meter to put in more coins or choose to risk a parking penalty.

- **Uncertainty of resources**. Also, the value from the experience is co-created. This means it depends on the balance of resources of the firm in its proposition, and on the resources accessible to the individual to co-create that value. This is the uncertainty of resources.

Example: your customer has a great imagination and believes the weather will be good BUT he thinks he may not have time to

attend the concert on that day. So £100 an hour is now worth £30 or less? Conversely, you might think a gym membership is worth buying because you overestimate your own conviction in sticking to a fitness regime.

- **Uncertainty of agency**. Sometimes, we don't buy something because we don't know if we want to use it in a particular context, even if we can use it. For example, at the airport, we may not buy the romance novel that we wish to read because we may be too embarrassed to be seen reading it on the plane with others looking on. So it's not that we don't have the resources or skills to experience an offering, but that we don't wish to act that way; this is an example of an individual lacking agency on context.

- **Uncertainty from the attributes and affordance of offering**. What can an object enable you to do? This is the affordance of an object. A chair is 'sit-able', a can of soda is 'drink-able'. We buy offerings because we believe in what they can enable us to do. Yet, there are times when we are uncertain if an offering can really enable a certain action.

> For example, a kite is 'fly-able' but even if you do know how to fly a kite, you might doubt its ability to fly because perhaps it is not well balanced. Since you cannot try it out at the shop, you can only take it at face value that it can 'do what it says on the box'. On the other hand, you might think that it is able to do more, and can imagine all the fun you will get from it, which increases the worth of the object.

These five uncertainties serve to explain why marketers have endeavoured to use all sorts of promotional techniques to persuade an individual to buy – teas, coffees, TVs, beds, flooring, drills, and BBQs. The persuasion often runs in the following manner: 'buy this because you get such-and-such benefit from it'.

Yet, when we examine this paradigm closely, we realise that the focus has been on how you assess worth, rather than on the value you create in context after acquisition. This is because exchange has traditionally been located out of context of value creation. The world makes you acquire almost everything before the context of use, i.e., advanced exchange. It also makes the assumption that ownership is the only way you can achieve some of your goals, enabled by these objects.

Must all resource acquisitions be out of context and in advance? Not necessarily. Given the differences in willingness to pay between in-context and out-of-context exchanges, it is natural to ask if there are other ways to achieve the outcomes we want. There have been recent business models that consider economic exchanges to occur based on outcomes.

## OUTCOME-BASED EXCHANGES

As the world moves towards ways to moderate resource depletion, it becomes obvious that as consumers, we do not all need to own the drill that is used only three times a year, a car in the city or even the baby items from ten years ago that are still sitting in the garage.

Where borrowing, leasing or buying from charity shops used to make consumers feel either like a freeloader or a miser, increasing pressure on shoppers to be green is now ushering a more 'feel-good' sentiment for such actions. This has increased potential for companies such as rentalic.com ('rent, share and be green') to bring together a community of consumers to share items that they don't really need to own. Such a phenomenon, known as collaborative consumption (Felson & Spaeth, 1978), isn't just happening at a local consumer level, but even with large organisations. By renting or leasing, consumers can buy what things can do, rather than the things themselves. In other words, the consumer buys outcomes/benefits – rather than ownership – of things. While the lease model has been around for sometime, the biggest challenge (and costs) has been to match what is available for whom and when. With greater connectivity, such costs could be reduced to a minimum, leading to a surge in collaborative consumption.

Engines produced by Rolls-Royce are maintained through a 'Power-By-The-Hour®' pricing mechanism, with Rolls-Royce selling propulsion (outcomes of engines) rather than the activities to service the engines (Ng et al., 2009a). The price for the maintenance, repair and overhaul service of the entire UK RAF Tornado fleet is based on BAE Systems's ability to deliver a bank of flying hours for the fleet, rather than on repairs and parts (Ng et al., 2009b; 2010). These are the ways in which some economic models are moving towards outcome-based exchanges.

Outcome-based exchanges between firms and customers are increasingly possible as a new business model. Such outcome-based exchanges focus on achieving a predetermined outcome instead of providing a service or a product. As an analogy to Levitt's *Marketing Myopia*, instead of paying for the ownership of a drill, we could pay for holes in walls (Levitt, 1960). Already, telcos are almost providing that option, asking if you wish to pay-as-you-go (outcomes) rather than pay in advance (prepaid).

The challenge for outcome-based exchanges is determining where to draw the line on outcome. Some outcomes are drawn very close to the value-creating context, e.g., paying for minutes of use after a phone call, for amount of water used, for amount of time the car is parked in the car park, etc. Some are drawn more widely, e.g., pay based on how many successful products created, and others even wider, e.g., no incidents in security service, winning a legal case, better health, or even paying for education only when you get a job. Outcome-based exchange is known by many names – cash on delivery, no-win-no-pay, no-cure-no-pay, payment-by-results, commissioning for outcomes, payment for progress, performance-based or outcome-based contracts.

From the digitally connected world perspective, so-called 'delivering' on outcomes (when outcomes are co-created, it's hard to think how a firm could actually 'deliver' on outcomes) is also starting to take shape in cloud computing. The 'cloud' provides firms with services without the need for them to own the technology infrastructure behind the services. Firms buy the ability to conduct complex computations, control payroll or manage databases without knowing or owning any server capacity.

Outcome-based exchanges are certainly seen to be more effective, if the firm and customer can agree on what outcome should be achieved. It aligns the incentives of both the firm and the customer towards the outcome. If you pay only when outcomes are achieved, you would feel that there is greater worth in the offering. If your accountant or your lawyer charged you by the hour, you might not be able to dispel the thought that they may not be working as efficiently, even if you do trust them. Similarly, if firms made money from your laptop or equipment breaking down, what is there to stop them from making equipment that won't last very long? This sort of behaviour, which economists would call opportunistic, is reduced once the firm is only remunerated based on outcomes.

Yet, despite its attractions, outcome-based exchange suffers from its own set of challenges:

**The determination challenge**. First, since the revenues for the firm come from outcomes that are the co-creation of value by the individual and the firm, the firm has no control over the customer's contribution. If it was really possible to pay for a hole in the wall, the drilling of the hole depends on the customer's capability. If the customer is not able to do it, is this a problem of the drill or the individual? Similarly, Rolls-Royce's 'Power-By-The-Hour®' earning revenues for each hour of engine in flight would depend on where the customer is flying (environmental conditions such as ash, sand, etc. have an effect), and the customer's ability to use the engine with due care (Ng et al., 2012). Determining an objective measure of outcome is a challenge.

Second, determining the boundary that is acceptable as an outcome is also fraught with ambiguity. After all, should the outcome of a good night's sleep be the measure of a good hotel room? Clearly, if the customer has a big job interview the next morning, but this would not be a fair measure of the hotel's service. Yet, if a hotel is truly able to provide a good night's sleep regardless of what happens the next day, that must surely be a great service! Outcome-based exchange therefore puts the challenge onto the firm in terms of its ability to achieve cooperation, collaboration and ultimately co-creation of value with the customer to achieve the outcome stipulated for the exchange.

Finally, outcome boundaries are infinite because they are nested within wider systems. Teaching me a new language could lead to an outcome of my being able to speak it socially, which could lead me to being able to speak it more formally, which in turn could lead me to teach the language to someone else. Similarly, being able to use my phone to make a call isn't just about the minutes I used, but about the message I communicated that led to some other outcome. As outcome boundaries go further away from the firm's role in value creation, it just gets harder to determine the acceptable boundary at which an exchange (payment) and an assessment of worth can be conducted.

**The measurement challenge**. Even if the boundary for the outcome is accepted, outcome-based exchange is faced with a measurement challenge. For example, if you taught English to a student, you might be confident in your ability and be willing to be paid according to every English word spoken after the lesson. Yet, how do you measure that? Short of recording the student 24 hours a day, this would be very difficult to measure. Also, what if the student is rather reserved and doesn't speak very much?

Research (Payne & Frow, 2005; Payne et al., 2008) has discussed the difficulty of developing appropriate metrics for value-in-context, stating that metrics to measure and monitor the conduct of the customer is underdeveloped. Of course, if the outcome boundary is based on a piece of equipment, e.g., an engine or an MRI scanner, it might be easier to adopt equipment use as an outcome measure but that is a *measure* of use, which is more dependent on the firm, rather than the *outcome* of use, which is more dependent on the customer.

So the readiness of a jet to fly ten hours could be an outcome boundary for the firm and is within its control, since the firm maintains and services the jet, but the actual number of hours of the jet's use to achieve a mission whenever the customer wishes would be the customer's preferred outcome. The assessment of worth for the firm's offerings therefore hinges on the boundaries to which both sides are agreeable.

**The revenue challenge**. Related to the measurement challenge is the revenue challenge. This is the challenge of assessing worth, given that the outcome of value creation is attributed both to the firm and the customer. If both sides are responsible for an outcome, who should be compensated, and what is the basis for compensation? The firm can argue that the set-up and infrastructure just to deliver energy to your home is immense, while you can argue that you should only pay for use and not for any of the set-up costs to get energy into your home. For economists, this is the age-old problem of transfer pricing (Wilson, 1993; Rochet & Tirole, 2003).

The UK Ministry of Defence have contracted the service of its fastjets to BAE Systems on the basis of cost per flying hour as an outcome and it has been reported by the National Audit Office that in doing so, it has saved £1.3billion, reducing the cost per flying hour by 51 per cent (Ng et al., 2013). Yet, it has also been shown in other research that a shift towards achieving outcome is not always profitable for the firm, because of the risks of the customer not doing their part.

**The context challenge**. Since value creation is contextual, the time and space of context are therefore uncertain. This includes the social, ecological and environmental surroundings at the point of experiential use, and while it may not be possible for the firm to control them, they would nevertheless be important factors that would influence the assessment of worth.

As the earlier example has shown, if the weather is not conducive to flying, then the firm may not get paid if the outcome is the plane in flight. This would suit the customer well but would not suit the firm which has already invested labour, capital and other costs in getting the jet ready for flight.

The context challenge is therefore a challenge of time and space of experiential use that could be uncertain, leading to inconsistent outcomes. Some research has shown that the contextual variety of use has become a serious issue for equipment-based outcome contracts, requiring constant amendment to contracts to accommodate increasing sets of contextual possibilities.

**The attribution challenge**. In the previous chapter, I argued that individual resources are central to creating value. This creates a resource challenge for assessing worth in outcome-based exchanges. Whose resources are required to achieve the outcomes? If they are part of the firm's offering (e.g., resources to bring energy into the home), this could be priced and the firm should then ascertain if it is viable to serve an individual's home.

But what of the customer's use of resources? Energy is useless on its own. Individuals have to buy electrical equipment to use energy – lights, ovens, fridges, TVs – and these devices are useless without the customer using them. The resource challenge is one of apportioning worth and attributing the outcome achieved to the value created with different offerings. This is not an easy task because our perception of goodness is not correlated to worth or money. For example, we may pay only 40 pence for a glass of water, but its goodness is worth much more than that in terms of our health. The assessment of worth for outcome-based exchanges is, therefore, having to confront the issue of attribution.

**The skills challenge**. If we return to the idea of paying for holes in walls, what happens if we do not have the skill to drill a hole in the wall? Outcome-based exchanges have to consider the customer's skill to create value from the offering. This of course is mitigated in advanced-based exchanges. If you do not know how to use a drill, you just either don't buy, or if you do buy it, then it's really your problem – and not the firm's – to get a hole in the wall.

In outcome-based exchanges however, it is now the firm's problem as well, because if the hole is not created, the firm doesn't get paid! Firms now need a completely different approach in segmenting their customers, so that only those who can drill may use it. Yet, this may severely limit the market. Instead, the firm may now need to consider changing its offerings to include ways to help you learn to use the drill. What this means is that the customer's skills and ability to access resources to co-create value becomes the firm's responsibility, if the firm is paid to achieve holes in walls.

Although outcome-based exchange could be possible, there is still a need for the offering to be in context, for value to be created before an outcome is achieved. This means that an advanced acquisition is still necessary, even if we are allowed to pay for it based on outcomes. For water to be paid according to use, you will still need pipes and water meters. To pay per use of a car (e.g., smartcar), you would still need to get hold of a car first.

From the firm's perspective, outcome and advanced exchanges mirror each other in terms of worth. In advanced exchange, the firm commodifies its resources (labour, capital, etc.) to create the worth of an offering, an object or a set of activities so that an exchange can occur. In the outcome scenario, a boundary or an objectively measurable outcome can also create worth to be exchanged for economic value. Exchange occurs when the firm's attempt to create worth (producing a product, service, co-creating outcomes) is assessed to be of some worth to the customer.

## CONTEXT-BASED EXCHANGES

It must now become evident that instead of advanced-based or outcome-based exchanges, there could be something in between.

Since value is created in context, is there not a way to create exchanges within it?

Firms tend to think of their offerings that we have purchased as value propositions that achieve outcomes and benefits for their customers, and indeed they are. For example, they will tell you that a juicer gives you the endless benefit of juicing fresh fruits that will help you live a healthier life, or that a board game gives you hours of entertainment. However, they tend to overlook two steps between the proposition and the benefit/outcome from the offering:

- the contextual experience that results in value being created as explained above; and
- the design of the context before you can experience it.

**Context design**. Whenever we arrange the things we have around our house or office, or decide what to pack in our luggage, put into our drawers or toiletry bag, we are designing the context of experiencing the objects we have acquired.

For any object to be a value proposition, it must be *available in context* even to propose value to be created. This means that the camera must be with you when you wish to take a picture, the printer ready and able to print the document when you need it, the apple in your bag when you want to eat it. This is the design activity of the individual and we do this every day, all the time.

This is also hugely underestimated by those who sell us things, because firms sell us objects based on their function and hardly ever look into their connectivity within a context. This is all well and good in the old world of manufacturing and service exchanges. However, in a digital economy of connected things, there is a need to understand how and why things are connected, usually through their use by individuals.

The need to understand contexts and their archetypes (i.e., patterns) is becoming more urgent. To do so, we must understand how individuals design contexts for value creation. Engineers are not the only professional designers. Herbert Simon (1996) considers that 'anyone who devises courses of action aimed at changing existing situations into preferred ones, is a designer'. As human designers, we therefore aim to engineer our context so that we can create value with the objects we have acquired, to achieve the outcomes we want. We place mugs in our kitchen probably near the kettle, the TV in front of a sofa, and pens all around the house.

Contexts are partially designed by the individual, dictated by social rules (carrying an umbrella in London), norms (having perfume in your bag), and sometimes regulation (carrying your drivers' licence with you), and partly emergent through the creation of socially understood templates (some men stand up when a woman enters a room).

It is not merely a matter of the firm identifying what the need is within contexts and the form that would fulfil the individual's need. It is also about finding ways to access the individual at the point when the need arises. Think of the time when you had run out of milk or shampoo, and you will recognise that despite our advances in technology, we still have to remind ourselves to pop out to the village shop or supermarket to get it. You could of course, order it online and on mobile as well, but it still takes time and few providers would deliver a carton of milk for free. In other words, serving contexts is costly for the customer, and because accessing contexts are different for different people, the variety to serve is high, and it is costly for the firm to put such systems in place.

Creating exchanges close to where value is created means creating exchanges in two places; during context design, and/or during the contextual experience. For example, say you are preparing for a dinner party and you need candles for the table. Assuming you haven't bought any in advance, there are therefore two ways to acquire them – if you realised this before the dinner party, you may be able to buy the candles and have them delivered to you before the party starts, assuming there is a viable channel for both you and the firm to create an exchange. However, if you realised this only during the dinner party, it may be too late for you to do anything about it as you would be in the midst of the party and could not possibly get out of it. In the former, an exchange is viable and markets are created. In the latter, an exchange may not be viable and we have market failure.

Creating exchanges that serve contexts is therefore a challenge. Exchanges could still be possible at the contextual design stage, but almost impossible during the contextual experience, especially for physical things (although this will change with digitised things). Baldwin (2008) gives us a reason for this. In her article, 'Where Do Transactions Come From?', she discusses the production system of a firm as:

> a network of tasks (that) allows us to model new patterns of
> dependency and interaction, including parallel flows of material
> and information, backward flows (feedback), and iterative and
> uncertain flows (trial-and-error). These more complex patterns
> cannot be modeled as a simple 'sequence of stages', but they do
> arise – frequently – in real production processes.

Baldwin describes the workings of an organisation which is almost exactly like the workings of a home, or a context of experience. More importantly, she describes such systems as a 'transaction-free zone' – a time and space where it is very difficult to intervene through an exchange, much like wanting to have candles while you're in the midst of your dinner party. Contextual experiences are therefore traditionally seen as transaction-free zones because many of the interactions within the zone are non-linear, dependent on different people doing different things, and uncertain. These interactions are what Baldwin calls 'thick crossing points'.

Using the energy analogy, we buy objects for their potential and can only realise this potential when we put them in place in context and experience them, i.e., when they become kinetic. So the transaction-free zone is the kinetic where the value is created, but buying some potential when you're in the midst of the kinetic is very difficult, because the cost to serve you is too high for the firm, if the object is in a physical form. Even if the firm can do it, you may find it unaffordable to buy. There are many times in lived lives where we wish we could have something and would gladly pay for it, but it is either too costly for the firm to access your context to serve, or to know what you need.

Digital offerings that understand the interaction between content and contextual exchanges could change this. Firms that provide digital content could create a thin crossing point in the kinetic by changing the way in which they are presented. For example, it is commonly known that if you wish to stream a live satellite telecast of a football game, the price to watch would be very high. If you are willing to stream the same game but with a five-minute delay, the price drops off a cliff. Traditional goods-dominant logic would consider the offerings as two different products sold at different prices to different customer segments. However, every football game has a half-time that lasts around fifteen minutes. What if the game was very exciting and the score was a draw? Would a viewer who bought a five-minute delay game be interested to upgrade to a live satellite telecast? If this option was available, the firm would have been able to create a context-based exchange within the kinetic of viewing the content. This could be done by creating modularity within the content, allowing for an exchange to occur. This is already beginning to happen with TV shows that allow for voting by audiences. The future of modular content to allow for context-based exchanges is only beginning.

Creating context-based exchanges will become more commonplace in the future when content, media and business models begin to collaborate. The challenge of new markets can be summarised in three factors:

- knowing when (context) there is a need for something (the resource requirement to create value);
- knowing the form in which that need could be fulfilled (the offering);
- knowing what activities, entities or issues exist within the value-creating context to create worth so that exchange can occur (the exchange).

These three factors epitomise the firm's business model for any offering. Osterwalder & Pigneur (2010) proposes that a business model has three components (see Figure 5.1):

- *value proposition*, i.e., what the customer acquires to create value with, which is the second challenge of new markets;
- *value creation* – this maps onto the first challenge which is knowing the context and the resource to create value; and
- *value capture*, i.e., creating worth so that exchange can occur.

Notice that when we separate the value created from worth, we can explain the various phenomena that we see in markets today. Traditionally, the offering that proposes value is the component in the value-creating system that creates worth. This means that the creation of worth (making a washing machine) is more or less aligned to the creation of value (use of washing machine through ownership).

However, we are now seeing more cases where the creation of worth is not the same as participating in the creation of value. A firm could contribute to value creation as a proposition, but may not be compensated directly for that proposition. For example, Google offers its search engine to many people in the world, but they do not 'pay'

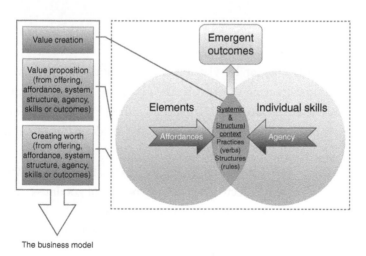

The business model

FIGURE 5.1: The business model and value creation

directly for Google's services. Instead, Google commodifies the customer's skills and agency (eyeballs and ad clicks), creating worth for the market of firms who wish to advertise to appropriate market segments that use Google's search engine.

Similarly, in outcome-based contracts, the firm may give an engine for free, and it creates worth from the outcome that is achieved from the value-creating system. This is what I mean when I say that the firm should always design an offering to participate in value creation or to propose value-in-context, but the way the firm creates worth from that value-creating system may be quite different. The firm could be creating worth from the ownership of its offering (the traditional route); it could create worth from what the offering does, i.e., its affordance such as the number of photocopies, the customer's skills (trust), the customer's agency (Google) and outcomes (better health). This will be discussed further in Chapter 9.

In short, *designing for value creation and creating worth for exchange are separate activities.*

The creation of worth for exchange and the design for value creation (service) will be discussed in the next half of the book as I consider the role of digitisation in shaping business models and exchanges.

## CHAPTER 5 REFLECTIONS

We started this chapter by visiting a cave – not just any cave but Plato's fictional creation illustrating the gulf between perceptions and reality. For the unfortunate occupants, confined at the back of the cave, their only realities were the flickering shadows projected onto walls.

In the same way we can now see that in relatively recent times, the notion of value has been reduced to a shadow of goodness that we call 'worth'. This diminution or downgrading of reality has, in the pre-digital era, been a reflection of the need for exchange – the drive towards 'putting a price on everything'; as the critic would say, 'but understanding the value of nothing'. However, a market economy still needs markets. Refreshing and reinterpreting the new realities in our digital economy – the values in context – raises many challenges and uncertainties.

Reinterpreting the meaning of worth – looking at how this might be achieved – is a worthwhile exercise and leads us towards the notion of 'outcome-based contracts'. However, despite obvious attractions, they in turn throw up challenges.

If value is co-created and therefore dependent on the agency of the customer, how can the firm find objective measures of outcome? And where are the boundaries of responsibility for performance? How will revenues be shared? What happens if, during the lifetime of the contract, the context changes? And what of the customer – the contribution to the outcomes of his own resources and skills?

Lying somewhere between traditional exchange and outcome-based contracts, we can envisage 'context-based exchanges' – although these too will have their own challenges.

There's a distinction to be drawn between creating worth at the point of exchange, from the firm's viewpoint, and, from a customer viewpoint, the co-creation of value-in-context – or what most of us call 'service'.

# 6    Rise of the digital economy

Digitisation is the conversion of analogue information in any form such as text, images or sound to a digital form so that the information can be processed, stored and transmitted through digital circuits, devices and networks. Digitising information makes it easier to store, access and share. In the old days, if you wished to see the front page of an old newspaper, you could only do so if you visited the library at the location where it was held. Today, you can often buy a back copy via the Internet from wherever you are, or at least access the front page and the stories within.

As a global system of interconnected computer networks, the Internet has catalysed greater digitisation and is now able to serve the digital appetite of billions of users worldwide. Any clever means of digitisation, whether it is of a book or our X-rays, can potentially be communicated and accessed by anyone through the Internet, subject to consent. Enabled by global acceptance of the Internet Protocol (IP), it is a network of networks – encompassing millions of private, public, academic and governmental networks, from a local to a global dimension, and utilising a diverse range of electronic, wireless and optical networking technologies.

Such an infrastructure allows the carriage of digitised information anywhere and everywhere, whether it is to send a simple message via email, or a long conversation through Voice over Internet Protocol (VoIP), or even when we seek entertainment through Internet Protocol Television (IPTV). Online shopping sales are now higher than traditional retail sales in the UK, and business-to-business supply chains and collaborations have reached new heights.

No industry is spared from the digital economy and its potentially disruptive effects, affecting some positively while others would feel its impact negatively. The weekly wage of an engineer in Bangladesh rose from US$2 to US$25 by working for companies around the world, thanks to companies like Odesk, the largest online workplace. In the digital economy, work no longer has to be in a physical place, and many people can work whenever and wherever they want, resulting in both gainers and losers.

The digital economy allows many to choose access rather than the ownership of things, taking the advice of environmentalists who have long encouraged the borrowing of things we only need occasionally. Zipcar and Hertz Connect allow you to carshare instead of buying a car, especially when you don't need a car all the time. You can now rent iPhones, party supplies, textbooks, sports and fitness equipment, camping gear, and even dogs and gardens. The growth of the rental market is very much aided by the Internet which has reduced the transaction costs of putting together rent schedules of things and matching renters to things. Such is the embrace of digitisation that in just two decades, it is difficult to identify any part of the economy that has not been impacted, and the pre-qualifier 'digital' may soon be considered redundant.

With digitisation, identity is now an industry – with firms profiting from protecting your privacy, reducing identity theft and authenticating who you are when it matters. Ushuaïa Ibiza Beach Hotel, in partnership with Barcelona-based biometric payment provider PayTouch, allows guests (who register upon arrival) to make payments with their fingerprints across all their facilities so that visitors do not need to carry wallet or cards. Data (and particularly *usage* data) is now the new currency as firms entice you to give more information on who you are, what you like and what you do so that they can be more precise in their segmentation, service and design of offerings.

What happens next? The way we digitally connect on the Internet is through an IP address – our laptops, mobile phones, routers and printers are all connected through an IP address. It is a numerical label assigned to each device participating on the Internet which serves two principal functions: identity (what it is) and location (where it is). Through the IP address, connected things can find a route for information to flow between them.

However, not everything that is connected needs a public IP address. Private networks such as an office intranet or equipment on a factory floor do not need an IP address for every device even if they are networked between themselves. An IP address is only needed if the device is connected to the Internet, which of course then takes advantage of search and other standard applications available on the Internet, rather than having to develop proprietary ones.

Public IP addresses are managed by the Internet Assigned Numbers Authority (IANA) globally and by five regional Internet registries (RIR), and they assign IP addresses to end users and local Internet registries, such as Internet service providers. IANA uses Internet Protocol version 4 (IPv4), a communication method and protocol to assign addresses to devices. Consider IPv4 as a language, location and identity method to enable things to talk and make sense to one another. IPv4 has provided approximately 4.29 billion addresses.

## HYPER-CONNECTIVITY AND IOT

On 3 February 2011, it was evident that the pool of unallocated IPv4 addresses was becoming close to exhaustion. A total of 4.29 billion addresses had been used up by existing devices around the world! Since an IP address is a crucial factor in connectivity and in the development of future products, Internet Protocol version 6 (IPv6) was launched. As the latest revision of the Internet Protocol, IPv6 can have $3.4 \times 10^{38}$ addresses! On 6 June 2012, more than 3,000 firms including Google, Facebook, Amazon, Wikipedia as well as network operators and home router vendors showed that they could deploy IPv6 successfully. IPv6 got the digital world buzzing about what other 'things' could be connected to the Internet and why.

Concurrent developments in the Auto-ID space such as RFID tags have created the potential to identify and connect normal things for 'real-time awareness' in an inexpensive way. An early exploratory RFID application saw these customisable tags embedded in the heels of upmarket shoes, enabling the shop assistants to be better informed when those shoes walked through the door again. Wireless sensor technologies allow objects to provide information about their environment, context and location; smart technologies allow everyday things to 'think and interact'; e-textiles or smart textiles are fabrics that enable digital components and electronics to be embedded in them. Even old things could be potentially connected. Surfaces could be coated with conductive paint; electronic polymers now allow for smart glass as the surface for mirrors; plastic electronics allow circuits to be produced at relatively low cost by printing electronic materials onto any surface, whether rigid or flexible.

With nanotechnology and energy-scavenging technologies packing more processing power into less space, the potential to connect everything old and new for innovation and economic growth sent the digital world into a creative tizzy. The term 'Internet of Things' coined by Kevin Ashton, a technologist and pioneer in the Auto-ID world, started to gain traction, and industry is starting to wake up to the possibility of every sector being even more disrupted by this hyper level of connectivity.

Yet, technology is not merely the reason why the digital economy is on the rise. Much of the buzz in technology circles remains within that field because there has been less discussion of how markets form from new technologies. Technology spurs growth and expansion but only when it is adopted by people and economic activity is created.

The pertinent question is: why have digitisation and the Internet become so prominent in our lives? How did this digital economy come to be and why? Only when we understand 'why', will we be able to understand the possibilities of what the future might look like.

Fundamentally, the digital economy exists only because we parted with some money to acquire the digital offerings. We have purchased e-books, subscribed to broadband, bought mobile phones with data plans, downloaded music, movies and podcasts. We bought software, tablets and laptop computers. We bought them because we assessed the offerings and deemed them worth buying as we could create some value with them to achieve our outcomes and fulfil our needs. It is therefore important to understand how some of these technologies become a part of our lived lives, so that we can understand how new offerings of the future could emerge to be part of our value-creating contexts.

There are four major reasons why the digital economy will continue to expand, which will be discussed in the following section.

## SERVING CONTEXTS

Traditionally, exchanges happened at retail locations. We bought what we needed from shops, whether they were just around the corner or required a shopping trip into town. As Internet access became ubiquitous, online shopping through the World Wide Web became commonplace. Yet, this still meant visiting websites in the same way we visited physical shops. Buying can therefore be viewed as an interruption to our lives (unless you are seeking retail therapy or window shopping). If we wanted something, buying it would be a 'cost' in terms of effort, to get what we really want – which is to use or experience it. Google became popular through its ability to match our search needs with websites, reducing such costs. Even so, it still meant that we had to buy in advance of use, whether from a shop or online.

Something else is now happening. Exchanges are slowly becoming closer to the contexts of use experience, even allowing us to choose how we wish to be served. We can now do our banking, watch the latest movie on demand and read our newspapers without leaving the house and without waiting too long to do it.

As more digitised offerings become available, we have switched our purchases from single-function items to a 'platform' that allows us to buy more digitised offerings to serve us in context. Our computers can now deliver a dictionary, an encyclopaedia or the opening cere-mony of the Olympics which we missed; our tablet/iPad can deliver our newspapers and books; and our mobile phone gives us the time, currency exchange, weather and a host of other services. Our TVs have now joined the fray and want to serve us on-demand movies, MTV, music and even golf lessons. As noted in Chapter 1, we not only make things that work; we now also make things that work with other things.

Many widgets in our homes will soon be the platform to serve up more services on demand, as firms begin to realise the strategic advantage of being a potential channel to serve you in your home. This includes fridge magnets: Dubai's Red Tomato Pizza allows customers to order their favourite pizza at the touch of a button. Members of the pizza company's loyalty programme are sent a free VIP Fridge Magnet which uses a smartphone's Bluetooth functionality to connect to the Internet. With a press of the button on the magnet, the pizza can be delivered to the customer's registered address.

What this means is that the separation between the acquisition and use of resources to create value is collapsing into a similar time and space. As my earlier chapter alluded, serving contexts is akin to mining for oil, with consumers often more willing to pay. Almost every item able to be digitised is vulnerable to this, and firms are looking for ways to better serve contexts through digitisation.

Little wonder that everything and anything that could poten-tially be digitised is being done so, giving birth to new services and offerings. Traditional industries such as newspaper, book and other print publishing are forced to adapt their offerings or risk being dis-rupted. With the proliferation of user-generated content such as blogs,

YouTube videos and online newspapers, often allowing access for free, the Internet has enabled and accelerated new business models, new forms of interactions and new ways in which we can live our lives.

The digital economy should therefore not just be seen from the perspective of the world of connected things. It should be seen from our perspective, our things, our communities and how we are empowered to take charge of these devices and connectivity to make things work for ourselves and to create value with these objects to improve our lives. This is important because a micro-perspective of our own empowerment is now able to be accommodated through digitisation.

Digitisation, as Normann (2001) puts it, enables individuals to create what he calls 'density'. Density seeks the mobilisation of the best combination of resources for a particular situation. Ultimately, density means that the customer has the world of specialist knowledge available when and where they like. Creating density is the fundamental driver to the digital economy. It separates technological innovations that will succeed from those that will fail. Density is the necessary condition for adoption and diffusion of innovation. More importantly, density implies pressure on firms to design their offerings such that they can be deeply personalised to create density.

To understand where new markets come from for the digital economy, we need to start with individuals. This 'outside-in' perspective is crucial for understanding the future of what could work and what might not. By taking this perspective, firms will strive to understand contexts of experience so that customers can be served better, especially with new technologies.

Serving contexts also means that firms can now create new business models of both ownership and access. For example, the market for luxury cars stood at US$350 billion total sales in 2011.[1] That is, however, the market for the *ownership* of these cars. Yet, there may be many out there who do not wish to own a luxury car, but would like to drive a Porsche on Mondays and a Rolls-Royce on Saturdays. If digital services in cars can help us detect where they are and what condition they are in, there could be a vast appetite for such services, assuming that technology allows greater viability to serve this market.

E- and m-health technologies are now able to collect your health data with real-time monitoring of vital signals so that care provision can be customised for each person. Where you are is now becoming more important than who you are, as location-based services are able to assist you, suggesting good restaurants, hotels and even discounts available in a new city or deliver your parcel to wherever you are. For their Chinese-speaking customers, stores like Harrods have a free Chinese language app with an interactive guide to the store, restaurant menus and details on events taking place.

Earlier in this book, I discussed why it may not be viable for the firm to serve milk to you at your home when you're running out of it, and that you usually have to go to the store to buy it. With improved technology we can now order it online from home, and when we buy is slowly edging closer to our contexts of use. For example, the Evian Chez Vous[2] website allows Parisians to order bottled water for direct delivery to their homes and businesses. In 2013, the service will be

---

[1] http://beforeitsnews.com/international/2013/06/market-of-luxuries-2460270.html. Accessed 1 August 2013
[2] www.evianchezvous.com/. Accessed 1 July 2013

accompanied by the Smart Drop; a Wi-Fi-enabled fridge magnet allowing members to order water automatically by pushing a button. It is not yet immediate, but it is coming very close to immediacy. The future of serving us in context is only just beginning.

## VISIBILITY OF THE SELF: EMPOWERMENT AND SERVICE

With all these changes, it is easy to think about how things have changed and how things could change further. Yet, fundamentally, it is also important to realise that human needs haven't really changed much. We still seek food, clothing, warmth, love, comfort, leisure and companionship, and we still wish to conduct our lives efficiently and effectively – but the form in which these needs have been fulfilled and the manner through which we have fulfilled them have changed markedly over the years. And they will change again and again over time. What is different, though, is visibility.

Before digitisation, we bought products and used them to fulfil our needs, gain benefits and achieve outcomes, but we did all that without much visibility to the firms. The firms only saw exchange, and occasionally when they decided to conduct a survey or run a focus group would they see what we did with the stuff we bought. As technology becomes more advanced, firms can see better what we do.

It is not a coincidence that there is now more talk about privacy than ever before. This is because much of our lives are now less private and more visible. With the ability of individuals to create density such that resources can be deeply personalised in context to create value, firms now also have the ability to 'see' how individuals interact around the products they have been offering. For years, banks could only interact with individuals when they called at the branch or on the phone. With credit cards and Internet banking, firms can now have better visibility of customers' activities around their use of money. In a similar manner, your cable TV provider is able to know what you like to watch and when. Interactions that never used to be visible, what I consider to be 'dark' interactions, are now becoming 'visible' or 'lighted' interactions.

A world of analytics and data mining has spawned from this visibility. Industry now wants to deduce more from the amount of data to which they have access; what they call 'big data'. According to IBM, we create 2.5 quintillion bytes of data, of which 90 per cent has been created in the last few years alone.[3] Yet, as the saying goes, a little knowledge is a dangerous thing. Despite the terabytes of data, current visibility only captures a very small proportion of lived lives, and the challenge is to draw the appropriate conclusions when we only have small insights.

For example, we may consider the healthcare industry as that which is transactional between individuals and their hospitals, carers, pharmacies and GPs. Yet, the biggest healthcare providers of children are their parents who look after them at home, making sure they eat their broccoli and get a balanced diet. These are dark interactions because there is no visibility of such interactions as yet. As the world moves to become more digitally connected (for example, the Wi-Fi-connected toothbrush) there will be greater visibility. This brings forward a greater need for legal frameworks as well as market systems around consent and privacy.

Aside from having more lighted interactions, we also volunteer more information about ourselves digitally. We tweet when we are unhappy, post pictures from our travels on social networking sites, and generally allow ourselves to be more digitally visible. The Internet, through social platforms, gives individuals a voice, resulting in firms being less dependent on market sector approximations and able to deal with millions of individuals who actively voice their opinions on their products, services and everything else. Our digital voices now echo across the world, creating challenges to firms who are not (yet) accustomed to such vociferous and empowered customers.

---

[3] IBM, 'What is big data? – Bringing big data to the enterprise'; www-01.ibm.com/software/data/bigdata/. Accessed 1 July 2013

Our digital visibility is also manifested in the way we are able to organise ourselves. Style and wardrobe apps on tablet and mobile phones can now help individuals keep a record of their entire wardrobe, matching looks and organising all their clothing, tagging them according to brands and colours. We can now organise not just our wardrobe but our wines, recipes, jewellery, games, films and books. We can track how deep our sleep is, be told when during a movie is a good time to go to the bathroom, and entertain ourselves with angry birds or a talking cat.

As a consequence of increasing channels for interactions, we begin to organise our lives so that we are empowered to do more and demand more. No longer content to be still, we feel it necessary to squeeze something (anything) into every minute of our lives. Sherry Turkle (2011) talks about the younger generation not being able to appreciate stillness, reflection and solitude. Our appetite for information, organisation and entertainment seems to be ever more voracious. With our digital selves becoming more visible, markets will find still newer ways to serve us, creating a spiralling growth of transactions and interactions in the digital space.

## VISIBILITY OF GROUPS: COLLECTIVE ACTION

Ribose-5-phosphate isomerase deficiency is the world's rarest genetic disease, with only one known patient. A rare disease is any that affects a very small percentage of the population. The Internet is like a digital soapbox that can now amplify the voice of patients, even when their affliction is limited to a small number. The Internet enables patient advocacy groups and healthcare providers to share data and find common resources to collectively find treatments.

The rise of digitised information and the Internet has therefore brought about greater visibility of like-minded people to each other, and many are eager to group together to share ideas, complaints and thoughts. Social platforms allow individuals to find one another and create advocacy or group platforms on Facebook, Twitter or LinkedIn. And instead of seeking advice from experts, opinions can now be 'crowd-sourced'.

The use of crowd-sourcing technology can potentially be contentious as exemplified by an anti-kettling app called Sukey. Sukey (as in the nursery rhyme 'Polly put the kettle on, Sukey take it off again') was developed with the aim of preventing violence at public demonstrations. The app allows protestors to communicate with each other during demonstrations and protests so that they can avoid being 'kettled', a controversial tactic practiced by law enforcers in the UK to confine demonstrators in a small area until they stop protesting.

Developed by students from the University College of London using Google Maps and open-source software like SwiftRiver, Sukey collects information on police activity from protestors on the ground, received through social media feeds such as Twitter and

Facebook as well as news from other conventional media like TV and radio. A live map is updated with the information, and with a clever combination of tweets, the map is able to simulate the movement of the police so that protestors can avoid encountering them. Sukey went live in London on 29 January 2011 during a protest against the university tuition fee hike, and it was reportedly the first out of five protests in the capital city at that time in which no protestors were 'kettled'. However, while Sukey's main aim is to keep protestors safe, it has given rise to debates about how the app may be misused for different purposes, such as instigating disruptive side protests.

The ability of groups to find one another and spur collective action, whether as advocacy groups or merely getting together online to share toddler tales has led to greater catalysis of the digital economy. Our ability to see, consult and discuss with one another through the Internet means we are starting to trust one another more than brands. The Nielson 2012 report[4] claimed that 92 per cent of global consumers say they trust word-of-mouth and recommendations from friends and family above all other forms of advertising, an increase of 18 per cent since 2007.

## DIGITAL BACKWASH

Digital backwash, as explained in Chapter 1, is when the act of digitising an offering to be made available on the Internet fundamentally requires a rethink of how the offering itself has to change. Most offerings that are information-based can be almost fully digitised such as music, books and photographs, and these offerings will feel the full impact of the digital backwash to an extent that can threaten entire industries. Yet, material offerings are not spared from the impact of digital backwash. Pervasive digital technologies can now enable products to be 'incomplete', with open and flexible boundaries

---

[4]  www.nielsen.com/us/en/insights/reports-downloads/2012.html. Accessed 1 July 2013

which can then allow both
the firm and its customers
to jointly design, redesign
and personalise the prod-
uct for use in customers'
contextual domains (Yoo
et al., 2012).

Take trains for
example. Even though a
physical train taking you
from London to Cam-
bridge could never be
digitised and offered on the Internet (you do need an actual train to
move from one place to another), creating value with a train service
usually means a high demand for information. Since the real challenge
for train travel usually lies in getting on the right train, what most
customers really want to know is which train they should get on, how
many seats are available on which carriage, where they can put their
bicycle/pram/luggage, and if they miss the train, which is the next
train they can take and can it be connected further south/north/east/
west? So a train service proposition is laden with demand for a lot of
information.

The 'digitisation' of a train service proposition could warrant a
redesign of trains, based on a completely different set of requirements,
allowing customers to personalise their train experiences. A train
could also provide informational resources for people away from the
train so that they can get onto the train, or to the concerned son
waiting for his father (who might need assistance on the train) to
return. Some of the information on trains is already available, e.g.,
through the UK National Rail phone app, which allows commuters
not only to see the schedules, but also the location of the train on a
map. This, however, is only the tip of the iceberg.

New materials for manufacturing trains and new ways of con-
figuring and digitising the train service could enable people to

experience trains differently. Surfaces, sensors and other material technologies could completely change the train experience, allowing commuters not only to know all the information of the train beforehand but to interact with each other as well. The information given to passengers and received from them could spawn innovative services to, from, and even within the journey itself, allowing for different types of revenue and business models. Because of digital backwash, the traditional train and the digitally connected train can be two very different offerings, and the market for train journeys could well extend beyond merely the commuters. This fundamentally allows the train company to derive revenues not merely through transportation of people, but from other customers who can create value from information about the train.

Digital backwash will impact offerings with high demand for information to buy and to use. At the exchange level, Amazon has already thrived on third-party reviews of the books they are selling being made available for others to see. You can also see the other types of products that may complement your purchase through the 'frequently bought together' feature on Amazon. Information for purchase is probably the most developed aspect of the digital world, with the Internet having been around for some time. Indeed, Google has developed algorithms to provide you with recommendations based on what you are likely to buy.

Information for use or experience is less developed, and this will be the next big wave of demand as digitisation moves to create services closer to contexts of use and experience. This will result in a better understanding of what information (and other products) is needed from the way things and people are connected in our lives. To a certain degree, every product can create a demand for information. A simple pen could have 'location' information or 'amount of ink' information. The questions are: how or why could the information be useful, for whom, in what context, should it be collected, and how?

French brand Babolat is launching the 'Play and Connect' tennis racquet with in-built sensors that can detect service speed, power of each hit and ball spin. It also monitors the type of stroke and the position of the ball on the racquet, enabling the player and coach to analyse both technique and game statistics. The data is sent wirelessly to a computer or smartphone, and players could set goals based on the data. It won't be long before technology will enable a barman to know that the beer is running low on your table, prompting him to come over to get a new set of orders.

Digital backwash and its impact on physical things is not just information about the thing; it, is also changing the thing itself by endowing it with other information, such as about its past. TOTeM (Tales of Things and Electronic Memory), a three-year research project, looks at how personal memories could be embedded with material artefacts, especially when the objects find themselves in charity shops. Oxfam's 'Shelflife' allows you to discover the stories behind items you find in Oxfam shops as well as share your own experiences of the items you donated to the shops. Similarly, ceramic designers and computer vision experts have explored how to create new ceramic designs that can track their history and use.[5]

The Universal Product Code (UPC) bar codes originally created to help supermarkets speed up the checkout process and to keep track of inventory is now being used to provide information on where the food is from and what its ingredients are. Even handbags are not spared. Vodafone UK and fashion designer Richard Nicoll created a handbag that can be charged through a power outlet, using a cable that magnetically attaches to the bag's exterior. After the bag is charged, it has two days' worth of extra battery to charge a mobile phone while on the move.

The forthcoming chapters will revisit value creation, value proposition and the creation of worth, and discuss how new markets are formed from digital connectivity.

[5] www.horizon.ac.uk/Projects/Trackable-Tableware. Accessed 1 July 2013

CHAPTER 6 REFLECTIONS

No discussion of the rise of the digital economy could start without a reminder that we are *not* merely talking about the ICT industry with its specialists in network development, devices and distributed systems. The impacts of digitisation are being felt in every corner of the economy – to the point that very soon this qualification, 'digital', will be redundant: whether impacted directly or indirectly, there will be no non-digital economy.

And if you have any doubt about this, look at the intense connectivity of sensors and robotically-driven devices envisaged (and being implemented) as 'the IoT'.

There are, we suggest, four good reasons why this is not some momentary disruption or passing fashion trend.

First, these new digital spaces afford or enable us to serve contexts. We want something but we do not want to shop for it physically. Exchanges such as shopping, all manner of services (like banking) and soon fabrication are moving closer to the context in which they are used and where the customer can co-create value. And all the time, the 'platforms', like the remote controller that you still persist in calling a mobile phone, and Internet services are bringing together offerings that can be blended and reblended in individual ways – shaped to suit your context. Deep personalisation is here to stay, because it makes our lives so much better.

Second, our embrace of the digital changes our visibility. Time was when a firm knew little or nothing of its customers, and even less of their experiences when using a product. Visibility was limited to the view across the counter. But now, not only do we volunteer more information about ourselves but the analytical tools to interpret and sift identities and behaviours provide huge opportunities to enrich the experiences.

And third, it is not just our individual selves that become visible. The habits of whole herds or groups of customers can be analysed in the cause of better design and more useful offerings. We may occasionally sense some discomfort from this exposure – we must defend ourselves against incursions into that which we regard as private. We may fiercely protect our medical records until that moment under the wheels of a bus when the context changes and we need full disclosure. We trade, individually and collectively, this visibility as part of the co-creation pact.

And finally, the circle is complete when 'digital backwash' impacts on the design of the offering. New products and services emerge, new markets are created, traditional offerings will be re-envisaged and relationships will be disrupted on account of our empowerment.

'Things may slide in all directions', but Leonard,[6] we will be able to measure them – more than ever before – and in every corner of the economy.

---

[6] *The Future* (1992), a music album by Leonard Cohen

# 7 Back to basics in value creation – a theory of latent demand

One shoe salesman reported back that there was no market because no one wore shoes. His companion reported back that there was a fantastic market because no one wore shoes.

Edward de Bono, Textbook of Wisdom

In Chapter 4, I discussed value creation as the experience of an offering. Since every offering is purchased, its experience is the firm's indirect (through the offering) or direct (through an activity or service) participation in the individual's value-creating activities and context.

Even so, where do we start in thinking about how *new* products could serve value creation in context? How should firms think about innovating their offerings to serve contexts better? How can we think about an offering before it exists? It is easy to decide post hoc, what needs are fulfilled by offerings we already know, but what about new things? To attempt to answer this question, we need to go back to basics in the domain of marketing.

Value creation for *new* offerings in the future cannot start with an assumption of what product or technology a firm already has. Instead, it has to start with what individuals might need.

Marketing has long discussed about how all products begin from needs (see Figure 7.1). We need food, shelter, clothing, comfort, friendship, but the way a need is fulfilled (therefore becoming a 'want') is a social and cultural expression. I might need food for breakfast in the morning, for example, but I would like (want) something spicy if I come from a different part of the world in contrast to my colleague who may just want toast. Demand is basically 'wants' that are endowed with buying power (Kotler & Keller, 2011: p. 816). I might want caviar for breakfast, but I don't have the means to afford it. Therefore, I am not part of the market demand for caviar.

Understanding innovation for a digitally connected future has to start by understanding needs, wants and then what might be demanded, which goes to the heart of how individuals currently live their lives. For new business models and how future digital products or services could become part of our lives, we have to understand fundamentally what our *latent* needs are.

FIGURE 7.1: Markets are fundamentally derived from needs

Since future digital services and products are enabled by connectivity, let us start with understanding existing connectivities.

## LATENT NEEDS FROM EXISTING SOCIAL CONNECTIVITY

We participate in many value-creating contexts in our day-to-day lives. If we take the example of the way we create value (goodness) from the objects around the home to achieve our idea of 'family', we see that we do this in our day-to-day practices (activity sets). These practices are expressions of our social and cultural values. Do we eat our dinner with our hands? Or do we use a knife and fork? Or a spoon and fork? How do we interact with our family members? Do we sit down for dinner and discuss the day, or do we watch TV together? These may be mundane day-to-day activities but it is in the mundane that our tacit cultural values are embedded.

It is also within these cultural and social values that we will begin to understand how we might need new things, or connect/converge existing things and buy from markets that would enable us to live our lives better. Understanding the mundane is therefore about understanding how we interact with each other and how we interact with objects that we have acquired. A parent may be cooking at an oven but could be doing so while his child is confiding in him what has happened in school. The existence of an oven timer therefore enables him to focus on his daughter's conversation, rather than keeping an anxious eye on the roast. Similarly, the football game on TV can be the means through which parents bond with their

children, and the fact that one can now record TV programmes enables them to watch a movie together at a time convenient to them all. Using Skype is now the way the extended family gets together on weekends, and this is enhanced by an occasional posting by one member of a link of interest on another member's Facebook wall.

It is through various objects and offerings proposed by the market that family members find new ways to interact in the digital age, to create their own ideas of what family is, and how they could interact. In fact, one could then say that certain objects in a household *enable* the creation and social construction of 'family', and the different objects within the context *afford* certain actions to be conducted as part of the value creation. The oven, the TV, the computer, the sofa; in fact, once you begin the list, you could include every object in a family home, and how it enables 'family' to be constructed.

Every object therefore has a story to tell, an affordance to act on which is a connected part of the family system; and every object offers *a service*, i.e., *a competency* to the system for different outcomes. Every object could therefore be seen as a resource, and we create value with it for the social construction of 'family' as an emergent property of a system.

Yet, an object is not always a resource. A TV is a resource in the context of the parents and children watching a game together, and an oven is a resource when the context is the parent and child conversing around dinner time. While objects are not resources all the time, our interest lies in the fact that they *are* resources at some of the time. If we start to look beyond the oven as an object of function (cook food) but as an object of affordance to enable certain actions that lead to the social construction of

a family, we can start to name a few of these family-creating contexts that include the oven. Here are a few:

- teaching a child to cook with an oven;
- chatting with family while cooking a meal.

If we now think of the oven not just as enabling the creation of 'family' as an affordance, but as enabling 'friendship', this list can be extended to:

- learning a recipe with a friend;
- friend borrowing oven to cook a roast;
- friends using oven to warm up food they brought.

In each one of the five contexts mentioned above, you could map out the verbs, nouns and rules of the context and start to visualise the value-creating elements around the oven in terms of what other objects it is implicitly connected to, the people it interacts with, and the way the oven is handled and talked about by the people embedded within the social and cultural ways we live our lives. Does that give you ideas on how we might wish the oven to be better? We can consider all objects within a context to render a service and we can map out the outcomes we hope to get from the context holistically, with one another. From there, we can understand where new needs might come from by understanding what type of resource may be inadequate.

This means that we are interested in the contexts in which the TV or oven are potential resources because when they are, people and objects become connected. Of course, they are not digitally connected (yet) but they are connected nonetheless, by the value creators i.e., the parents and their children.

This also means that the starting point in understanding latent needs or why we might need digital connectivity must begin with the understanding of the context of value-creating systems, because within these contexts, objects and people are already connected! Many of our non-commercial interactions, the dark interactions, give us a clue on where future exchanges could come from to serve life better, and assist firms to design smarter offerings and reduce potential failures.

As an example, take a look at the healthcare industry. It is a multi-billion dollar industry comprising transactions with pharmacies, hospitals, medical equipment providers, carers, patients and more recently, mobile and e-health organisations. While one would look at the healthcare industry in this manner, it really doesn't give us any sense of where the future of healthcare might be. One way is to think about health and well-being from an individual's perspective without only focusing on commercial interactions. That means that parents are the biggest healthcare providers and they are also the biggest well-being providers, merely by ensuring their children eat a balanced diet, taking care of them when they are ill, etc.

Yet, these interactions are not seen as part of the healthcare industry unless the parents bought some pharmaceutical products. It also means that when looking at healthcare and well-being holistically, we are missing a big part of the picture – that which we are already doing. To understand how future technologies could change or intervene in healthcare and well-being, we must therefore understand the healthcare contexts through which practices and interactions currently exist, and understand how they could be improved, i.e., healthcare as interventions in value-creating systems. With digitisation's ability to serve contexts better, the way to understand future digital markets would be to derive insights from what is currently non-digital and where digitisation could intervene since technology liberates us from constraints of:

- time – when things can be done;
- place – where things can be done;
- actor – who can do what; and
- constellation – with whom it can be done (Normann, 2001).

## LATENT NEEDS FOR INFORMATION

The second aspect of understanding where new needs could arise from digital technologies is to think about the nature of the digitised intervention itself – its capacity to serve latent needs. All digitised interventions are about the latent needs for information, possible information requirements and architectures around these latent needs. This means understanding what individuals do not know but would want to know, since their actions are dependent on this information. For example, Boondoggle's Winter Wake-Up alarm clock app wakes people earlier than usual if there has been unexpected snow or icy conditions during the night. This is because you might need more time to shovel snow from the front of the house or scrape ice off your windscreen, and if you have a meeting the next day, waking up early would be useful.

Comprehending information architecture gives us an understanding of how information can be represented, categorised or accessed to support its use. Yet, information architecture design often deals with data that is already in existence. What is more interesting is to think about the information needed to serve contexts. It really isn't hard once you think about it. Most systems analysts would look for information requirements in terms of what and when the information is needed so that they can design the 'how'. However, many people talk about information as though time has stood still when actually, time is always passing. I find it easier to think about the demand for information in terms of the temporal needs of individuals, i.e., information for future contexts (to plan ahead), information for present contexts (to decide, do or make things happen) and information for past contexts (to monitor, control or know about what has happened).

As humans, we have huge demand for information at all times. We wonder what the Sunday opening hours are for our neighbourhood supermarket, we would like to know how warm a cup of tea is, how cold it is outside and even the name of the artist singing on the radio. Shazam, a music app, 'listens' to a song and presents you with its name and that of the artist. Information needs from individuals often come in contexts and as we move through contexts. If we analyse contexts of value creation from the perspective of time, movement and place and then map them onto the demand for information, we can anticipate the information requirements of contexts and the possibilities for digitising the offerings already in contexts, or present new offerings to serve contexts.

## LATENT NEEDS FROM CONTEXTUAL VARIETY OF EXPERIENCE (CVE)

Earlier chapters have explained that value creation is achieved through the individual pulling in and integrating objects and offerings as resources within a context. If you consider objects within a context of a home, you could have a book, a music player and a TV; integrating these resources may achieve the outcome of a relaxed weekend. As things become more connected and more mobile, objects that we are used to having in one place can now be used in several other places. This has happened with music players becoming iPods and TV shows accessed through laptops; other objects are likely to follow suit.

From the perspective of these objects, the context in which value is created by the individual begins to exhibit what I call 'contextual variety'. This means that the 'service' of the object often takes place in more than one location in terms of time and space. Once an object is moved, it may no longer be a value-creating resource in a different context. For example, the laptop computer may be fully enabled to stream TV shows at home but will not able to do so on a train unless there is onboard Wi-Fi connectivity, thereby impeding the individual from creating value with it.

I consider offerings that create value with individuals across different spaces and times as exhibiting *contextual variety of experience* (CVE). It is the degree of heterogeneity or variability in the set of contexts within which the individual creates value through continual use of an offering. For example, an individual listening to music on his iPod not only on train journeys, but also in the gym during exercise, and/or while having lunch, would exhibit a higher CVE in creating value with his iPod than another individual who only listens to music before bedtime.

Why is this important? It is important because the connectivity of other things within the context changes. An iPod in a gym is connected (through the individual) to the treadmill, the gym's air-conditioning and the water cooler. An iPod at bedtime is connected (through the individual) to the curtains, bedside table and lamp. The CVE of an object therefore highlights other connected offerings or resources that make a difference in creating value with the offering itself for the individual to achieve the same outcome (listening to music). This means that contextual variety could give firms clues to innovating or increasing the connectivity of the offering (iPod) in future.

CVE can come about due to environmental conditions or the individual's personal conditions. In other words, context is not defined by the entities, but by the linkages and interactions between them. These linkages and interactions would be dynamically changing when an offering exhibits high CVE, as a consequence of individuals appropriating different resources in such contexts to achieve the outcomes they require. For example, when the newspaper was only available in print form, we would perhaps read it in the morning, over a cup of coffee at the breakfast table. Now, more people are reading them on trains as they are able to access them electronically. When newspapers became digitised, a latent need emerged as we realised that many people like to talk to other people about the news as they read them. Sharing online news as we read them over social platforms such as Facebook or Twitter is now common practice. If only the online newspaper could get us coffee, that would certainly make the experience complete.

CVE in the use of objects is increasingly pervading modern society, as individuals seek more resources to integrate to achieve multiple roles and tasks within their daily lives. Technological innovation in the form of smartphones, tablets and other handheld devices and their associated Appstore libraries have resulted in greater integration and interconnectivity, creating new resources in contexts and allowing individuals to be more productive and achieve outcomes in more varied conditions. In doing so, more latent needs emerge.

Today, one could read a local newspaper globally, share presentations, have group meetings in virtual spaces and allow a stay-at-home parent to do the accounts of a corporation halfway across the world. The CVE of many objects have increased, resulting in hyper-variety of use, and some firms have responded by modifying their offerings to allow for multiple contexts. In particular, healthcare products such as dialysis machines are starting to leverage on technologies to allow patients to get treatment within their contexts.

## LATENT NEEDS FROM RESOURCE CATALYSTS IN CONTEXTS

Innovative offerings are the new or changed potential resources in an individual's life. Whether it is a new washing machine, car or even pen, we tweak and design the contexts of our day-to-day lives to accommodate the new things we buy, often because we want to. So the most logical question to ask is – why would we want to? The traditional marketing answer is that 'there is a need'. While that is true, it is a most unsatisfactory answer because it begs a further question: what brought about that need in the first place? Creating value with something new in our lives is not without disruption. We need to learn how to use a new laptop, a new mobile phone, a new oven. Why do we buy them if they disrupt us? In other words, why are we willing to change our behaviours to accommodate the use of a new offering?

There are three reasons why we want to change our behaviours, either to accommodate new potential resources or to get rid of old ones. I call these reasons the *context catalysts* because they trigger the need for new or changed resources to create value, causing disruption to the context:

- First, human behaviour changes when there is a *pull effect*, i.e., something that makes the situation better, makes us better off, or makes the value-creating system *more viable*. This usually means the context is improved through the way we can create more goodness/value, e.g., having a game on the iPad to distract little ones while their parents are busy chatting after dinner.
- Second, human behaviour changes when there is a *push effect*, i.e., *a stress* to the situation such as a blackout in the middle of dinner.
- Finally, we change our behaviours when we know the *practice or process of change*, i.e., we know what to do, we've seen others do it or we mimic what others do. Sometimes this could be a conscious change because of the push or pull effect, and sometimes it could be unconscious.

This final cause for change is the most important because even if you suffer a push or pull effect, you would be like a deer caught in the headlights if you did not know what to do. You freeze and take no action. This is the *agency* that I referred to earlier – it is the capacity to act in a particular situation. Consider the very first person who ever ate a lobster. Given its hard shell and hostile demeanour, a lobster is

very difficult to catch and
that person must have been
hungry. It could not have
been that there was no
food, but perhaps there
was no food within his
context which then created
a stress in the system, trig-
gering a need for resources.

The ability to inte-
grate new resources and
have agency to change our lives is therefore contingent on these
context catalysts. Through them, we improve our own skills and
competencies to assemble and reassemble potential resources to
create value. We learn how to use the computer, the tablet. We learn
to programme the DVD player, and use Facebook or Twitter to
acquire additional resources to achieve the outcomes we want,
whether catalysed by push, pull or process effects.

Yet, resources are more than merely task-based resources. They
also include our own emotional resources. We must feel that music can
enable us to achieve emotional outcomes such as 'being happy' – so we
actively go out and buy music. Those who are more prone to depression
will understand why some people lack such emotive resources, which
makes it hard for them to create agency and be happy. Objects around
us help us activate emotive resources (e.g., old photo albums) which are
so important to achieve the outcome of being happy.

Focusing on value creation would also allow us to understand
better the convergence of things. Human behaviour is changing, with
new types of devices and new services. Some are adopted while others
are not. These new services give individuals access to information and
resources across different times and locations. This results in network
operators, broadcasters and content providers coming together in a
single market space. Firms traditionally in different sectors are now
competing with one other, creating new market dynamics and rivalry.

One way of understanding these dynamics is to shift the focus of analysis and insight to contexts of value creation.

The understanding of value creation in context also compels the firm to understand customer needs and usage requirements across differing environmental conditions better, so that customers are able to realise the firm's value proposition through their part in the co-creation process. In so doing, customers' use and achievement of outcomes could result in changing the firm's business model (Ng et al., 2013). Customer usage could result in different types of access rights to tangible goods and intangible activities within a service system – for example, hybrid revenue models of ownership/lease of goods and privileged access to activities and physical locations.

## FROM NEEDS TO WANTS: DE-INSTITUTIONALISING EXISTING SOLUTIONS

Understanding where latent needs might come from isn't enough. We also need to know how needs translate to 'wants'. 'Wants' are the *form* in which the needs are satisfied. We may need fluids but the form in which we prefer to satisfy that need may be water, soft drinks or beer. Products and services are therefore the forms through which needs are met. They are *solutions* to a problem that an individual faces, or a 'job to be done' as Christensen and Raynor (2003) would put it.

So a juicer juices fruits because a human being isn't able to do so as easily. A product or an offering is therefore touted to be a 'bundle of benefits', but the form and shape of this bundle could change. You could get a dictionary from the shelf or by going to dictionary.com on the Internet. These are two very different forms for serving the needs of individuals and yet achieving similar outcomes. As human beings, we accept an offering as a solution only after seeing it being used or using it ourselves. Only when we believe that our needs are met by a particular form (an offering that is either a product or service), do we believe that it is a solution.

Steve Vargo, who proposed the S-D logic, has spent some time thinking about this, and he considers markets to be *institutionalised solutions* because offerings that have markets are not only solutions – it has been accepted that the solution is of the shape, form and functionality of the offering in question. This means that markets are created from offerings that are of a shape and form that has become a social norm, i.e., the solution has become *institutionalised*. Only when the solution has been institutionalised will there be a market for it, meaning that only when the solution is accepted as a norm is there a demand for that offering that rendered the solution.

For example, if you need to know the time when you wake up in the morning, the form by which the need is satisfied is probably a bedside clock. Many people accept that this is the most common form of satisfying that need. Bedside clocks therefore become the institutionalised solution to the 'what-time-is-it-when-you-wake-up-in-the-morning' problem. Markets are created from institutionalised solutions, so there is a market for bedside clocks.

Institutionalised solutions, by nature of being institutionalised (i.e., have become a norm) create a huge challenge for innovators, because it is hard to think of other possible solutions when you are within an institutionalised mindset of knowing what a solution is supposed to look like. To jolt you out of that mindset, it would take a sudden realisation, for example, that you do not need a bedside clock if you had a

mobile phone which can also give you the time if it is by your bed. You could have come to that realisation due to the context catalysts; perhaps because your clock was out of order and you reached for your phone instead. In that process, you de-institutionalise the mindset of the solution, and accept that your phone may be your new bedside clock. De-institutionalisation is therefore a crucial key to accepting new interventions and offerings in our lives.

Objects that surround you may have the upper hand in creating new digital resources for the individual; this is what I consider to be the *contextual incumbency advantage.* White goods (fridges, washing machines), mirror surfaces, set top boxes, TVs and electrical appliances that exist at home could connect with each other to serve contexts better if they knew what our latent needs are. These incumbents are often already in context to serve, so the adoption probability of new services offered through them are higher and de-institutionalisation may be a lesser hurdle. This is why the smartphone has managed to become the new solution in context for previous solutions such as bedside clocks. It was an incumbent already present within our contexts.

## A SOLUTION THAT DOESN'T YET EXIST: EFFECTUAL REASONING

We search for new forms that could ensure that our needs are satisfied, especially when solutions do not exist. Human beings are therefore not merely context designers, we are *effectual* designers. Effectual logic is a different sort of logic from causal logic. Causal logic is about starting with a predetermined goal and a given set of resources or means, by which we seek to find the optimal (fastest, cheapest, most efficient) way to achieve the goal. Effectual logic, however, starts with having no specific goal but instead, with a set of means; by appropriating different resources, goals could emerge contingently over time through imagination and aspirations (Sarasvathy, 2001).

Sarasvathy provides a good example of the difference between causal logic and effectual logic. Let's say you have been asked to prepare dinner. You can do it in two ways. Through causal logic, you can decide that dinner will be coq au vin, go out to the supermarket to buy all the necessary ingredients in the most efficient and effective way, and proceed to make dinner. However, if you wish to use effectual logic, you won't decide what dinner would be. Instead, you throw open your larder and fridge, and based on whatever is available, some kind of dinner emerges. This is the logic often used by entrepreneurs.

Effectual reasoning differs from causal logic in three ways. First, effectual reasoning works on the principle of 'do not predict the future – invent it'. Second, it works on the 'bird in hand principle' which means not waiting around for the best opportunity, but just going for it with what is available in the present. Finally, effectual reasoning also works on being flexible and open to possible serendipitous opportunities.

Effectuation is the inverse of causation. It begins with given means, and seeks to create new ends by inventing and allowing a future to emerge through our actions of appropriating means and potential resources. Much of how we live our lives is causal, but when the situation is uncertain, we often rely on effectual reasoning. When we design a dinner party, we use causal logic, putting together all the objects that we have acquired so that value can be consummated between the individual and the offerings acquired. Yet, we also often see effectual context design, for example improvising with the use of a paper napkin when there isn't a plate, placing our jacket on the grass to sit on it, or in another setting, placing books underneath an overhead projector so that the image projected is at the right place.

Effectuation provides useful design principles for transforming our existing contexts into new futures. We should marvel at our ability to look at objects and decide what they can afford – whether it is what they have been designed to afford or otherwise. We use such reasoning to decide on the form which would satisfy our needs. Most times, we try to

be better designers and we prepare objects that are naturally available or have been acquired, so that they can be appropriately placed to create value at the appropriate time. Anyone who has ensured that the beer is chilled so that it can be taken out and enjoyed during a football game has designed a context to create value with the TV, beer, sofa and snacks. Getting friends to come over at the last minute to watch the game with you is just another step in context design to achieve the form in which our needs could be satisfied.

As our lives become busier and we start relying on more mobile objects, contexts become more uncertain; so much so that this has an impact from the perspective of emergence of goals. If context is dynamic and heterogeneous, and technology assists the individual to achieve different outcomes in context, the goals of individuals in such hyper-variety contexts may not be known in advance. As an example, consider an individual looking at sofas in a shop who would like to consult his wife. He then decides to take a photo of a sofa and emails it to his wife at that moment for her opinion. Both the technology (app) and the individual's own resources to be integrated for value creation are familiar, although the context may be different or new. With greater digitisation and interconnectivity of technologies encroaching into various aspects of individual lives, we could be empowered to achieve outcomes in more varied contexts and have different out-comes as well (Ng et al., 2012).

For urban dwellers, contexts of mobile digital technologies often exhibit hyper-variety – with city folk using mobile phones in varied situations. In the earlier example, neither the app (camera) nor its use is new; yet the goal emerged in a new context and the individual has to form the awareness of being able to create value from a resource that is available in context, and that he has the means to achieve an outcome of consulting his wife at that moment. This means that individuals' use of mobile digital technologies is highly driven by effectual reasoning. This impacts on how services become adopted and make a difference in our lives, as we search for new resources to make our lives better, and we find new forms that would satisfy our needs and new solutions for our emergent contextual problems. This is compounded by greater stresses to context (the push catalyst), resulting in us seeking out new or innovative resources to create value for different outcomes in varied contexts.

Thinking about probable offerings for latent needs requires an effectual logic, as well as a mindset willing to be de-institutionalised; both would trigger the design of potential offerings to serve contexts. 'Jobs to be done', to understand where needs are, is a rational logic. We may not necessarily know what the job is that needs to be done. If we knew what the questions were, and therefore what the needs were, we might think of how we can satisfy them. New solutions are therefore very tricky because we do not know what question to ask to relieve the stress in the system, or make the context more viable. In this sense, design thinking can be beneficial. But thinking about it effectually can help as well.

## ACCOMMODATING NEW SOLUTIONS: CREATING MODULARITY

In Chapter 5, I described contextual experiences as transaction-free zones because they are full of thick crossing points. Contextual experience is the kinetic, and it is hard to intervene with new resources. Thus, even if as individuals, we are effectual and want new solutions to satisfy our latent needs that have emerged, we may find that very few offerings will come our way since firms will not know we need them.

Interventions are not easily successful because value-creating contexts are 'messy' in the kinetic. They consist of multiple practices

and interactions that are very difficult to intervene in. Take for example, the context of a father and mother with a newborn at home. The interactions within that context are multiple, messy and non-linear because the actions of one person are dependent on the actions of the other. This means there is no sequentiality in the practices of all three individuals within the context that we can know of beforehand.

In such cases, it is difficult to create transactions to intervene. However, if you look closely at the context, there are several 'solutions' or products that have been put in context that do intervene, such as a cot, nappies, milk bottles and clothing – offerings purchased by the parents to ensure that they have the right resources to tend to their baby. These are the forms through which their known needs are satisfied. If there wasn't a cot for example, the baby could be sleeping anywhere – on their bed, on a mattress, etc. And the decision on where to put the baby to sleep is likely to be unstructured or uncertain because it may depend on where they happen to be in the house.

By buying a cot, the parents have *modularised* their context to accommodate the resource intervention. What is modularisation? It is the breaking up of one big whole into parts, i.e., breaking up one project into sub-tasks and functions, or breaking up space into sub-spaces. Modularisation helps human beings cope with the messiness of contexts. For example, instead of thinking about cleaning the whole house, we break up the task into parts so that we can either pass them on to someone else to clean, or have a systematic process to clean so that we don't miss parts of the house. In the case of the parents, instead of letting the baby sleep anywhere, they will structure their lives and their practices around putting the baby to sleep in the cot, perhaps in their bedroom.

This suggests an important point. New offerings or interventions in context must consider that the value-creating individuals within the context are willing to change in some way to modularise their practices, so as to accommodate the intervention and integrate the resource into the value creation context. In other words, in creating 'wants' that satisfy our needs, we modularise ourselves so that the form in which these wants that satisfy us (the product/intervention) can be accommodated in context, in order for us to create value with it. This accommodation creates a 'thin crossing point', i.e., a boundary so that a potential resource could intervene. The readiness of individuals to modularise their practices such that thin crossing points for new interventions could occur, is therefore an essential step towards acceptance of a new offering in context, and in turn creating new exchanges from the offering that could lead to new markets.

Hence, for an individual to create value from context, any new or innovative offering must include the individual's practices around the offering within the context. This means that the individual has to *change* what he or she does to accommodate the potential intervention, as the system (which includes the individual) will be better off because of it. Often, researchers and practitioners in analytics make the assumption that people are passive and that behaviours don't change when in fact, mere information of how we behave often changes our actual behaviour.

## FROM SOLUTIONS TO MARKETS

Just because there is one particular solution to a latent need does not immediately imply that a market is formed. There are many solutions out there that suit some of us, but they may not develop into a viable proposition because the solution did not become *institutionalised* (i.e., the norm) for markets. Institutionalisation of solutions is basically the diffusion of a practice (e.g., the value creation practices with an offering) to a wider audience. In Rogers' widely-known definition, diffusion occurs when 'an innovation is communicated through certain channels over time among the members of a social system' (Rogers, 1962).

There are several proposals of how diffusion occurs. Those from the relational models school of thought believe that diffusion increases or decreases with the levels of interactions between the practices and future adopters. So when a practice is socially meaningless, e.g., the spread of a disease, then the interaction does not have to be close – merely being in a physical space is enough to spread it. When adoption is socially meaningful, however, individuals develop shared understandings, and diffusion occurs because of the consequences of practice through each other's experience.

*Exchange dependence* is also thought to increase general diffusion. If teachers are dependent on students and vice versa, some practices that are innovative or solutions that are adopted (e.g., a new pen) could diffuse faster. *Cultural ties* between individuals belonging to a common group or social category also increase diffusion, as does *rational mimicking* where, when individuals have to conduct similar practices (e.g., making tea), diffusion could foster a new solution in this manner, or at least would compete towards doing it better. Another possibility is *theorisation*, a conscious development of 'why' a particular solution is adopted. If a particular child-rearing practice is adopted that improves the social and intellectual development of a child, such a practice would diffuse quickly. Strang and Meyer (1993) suggest that modern society would accelerate the adoption of possible solutions quickly because of *homogeneity* of individuals in society. We are increasingly drawn to mimic each other's lifestyles and subscribe to common collective standards. This means that when one person adopts something that they consider of value in its practice, it becomes rapidly institutionalised due to the similarities between ourselves as we become culturally similar in our embrace of modernity.

In the digital world, a digital service that is adopted could spread quickly through communities who are highly digitally connected, as testified by the Angry Birds game. This book will not go into details of product diffusion, but readers are most welcome to delve deeper into this phenomenon that has been subjected to much attention by adoption and diffusion researchers.

In the next chapter, I turn to viewing value creation from the perspective of the firm, and discuss how value propositions could be developed to intervene in lived lives.

## CHAPTER 7 REFLECTIONS

The focus for this chapter is central to the entire book. We are looking at markets and how they emerge from the needs of potential customers. 'Demand stimulation' is often woefully misinterpreted by firms whose marketing efforts may claim to start with the needs of customers, but are rooted in the products and services already offered.

New offerings, to serve 'value creation in context' (the needs, wants and emergent demands that define new markets), cannot be envisaged as a marginal upgrade to pre-digital products – no matter how much the firm would wish for a smooth incremental transition.

But if understanding innovation must start from understanding needs and wants (and then demand), how can we spot latent needs (those unfulfilled) within the complexity of our existing social connectivity?

Part of the answer lies in mundane observation of everyday life – the way in which some products enable inventiveness in their use and the co-creation of value.

It could be but a small step from the novelty of a digitally connected fridge magnet that, when pressed, reorders a specific product, to an entire fridge door that serves as the kitchen's online food shopping platform. Every object has a story to tell – the story of what it affords. These affordances provide contextual insights into the when, where, how, who and with whom, or what of digital liberation – or what so often dawns on us as the removal of everyday hassles in the way we work and live.

Another part of the answer lies in the latent needs for information. Here we are back again to that sense of interoperability – the things that will work better when enjoined to work with other things. The digital enablement of information fusion makes possible the alarm clock that is triggered by a time setting that is nudged by temperature to allow planning ahead for a commuter's snow-clearance.

And yet another facet of these insights into needs is influenced by a product's place-specific or place-generic characteristics – hence the huge interest in mobile apps and our new-found abilities to do different things in very different places. Can you order your groceries for home delivery when sitting on a hotel bed the day before the long flight home?

We all now do things that our parents would find very strange. Our children will find likewise. From this mix of a variety of contexts and our digitally liberalised inventiveness, new markets coalesce around those behaviours and practices that we copy and share – a process that is itself enabled by the extraordinary ease of digital connectivity.

# 8 Value propositions and new business models

People don't want gadgets anymore. They want services.

Jeff Bezos, 2012

While value creation (in use-contexts) is the cornerstone of future markets, it is still a relatively new concept for firms to understand. It's all well and good to describe value creation as part of the customer's constellation and space, but how should firms deal with this understanding of value creation? How should it change what firms do?

If we are serious about helping firms create new offerings to serve our needs, we need to persuade them what these offerings are and how they should be designed and made in the first place. Also, how should firms derive revenues from these new offerings? To answer these questions, we have to understand how offerings could be designed to be viable and profitable as well as fulfil our needs and enable better lives.

Too often, I hear firms being given advice on how to be customer-centred, but not enough on how they can remain viable in doing so. We forget that there are more than six billion people in the world, and all of us could be very different in the way we create value in our multiple contexts. If the firm wants to serve every one of us, and yet allow us to personalise deeply the offering for our own outcomes, the variety embedded into the design of the product and service would probably make an offering unviable.

Marketing has always advised firms to segment their markets before targeting and positioning their offering, because firms can't sell to everyone. This is fast becoming old hat in a digital economy because it assumes the product or service has already been created, and the task ahead is to choose a customer segment which would want it. With today's technologies, products and services could be designed, redesigned, created and recreated in modular ways very quickly, and tweaked to allow different ways of personalisation. In other words, firms can design an *incomplete* product, so that it is only completed and personalised by the customer, e.g., through a digital interface such as a smartphone. Thirty years ago, a PC came with preset specifications, and once manufactured, could not be changed quickly. Today, a tablet could update its operating system to allow multiple new functionalities. Also, 3-D printing and rapid prototyping allow more experimental products for those who are more adventurous in creating value in 'wilder' contexts. The boundary between the physical and the digital is becoming ever more fluid. This could completely change the way we think about manufacturing and design in a connected digital economy.

While there are aspects of the equipment that cannot be changed, the issue is: what should or should not be changeable to achieve increased revenues, high market penetration as well as deep personalisation? While it may still be true that a firm cannot sell to everyone, not being able to sell to everyone because not all can afford it is a different excuse from not being able to sell to everyone because the firm is not capable of serving their needs. With digital connectivity remodularising the offering, fragmenting and transforming content, material and information, a firm can rebundle its offerings to serve different customers at different times and different contexts. A train may only be able to take 300 passengers, but information about the train, its journey and the spaces on it could be a service scaled to serve millions who might want that information.

Understanding deep personalisation for value creation by a customer in a manner that can still ensure that the offering is viable and profitable is a major cultural change for many firms. To begin with, firms have to get to grips with a few changes to their mindsets.

### MINDSET CHANGE I: CUSTOMER AS COMPETENCY OF THE FIRM'S VALUE PROPOSITION

The first is the shift from thinking of firms as selling and delivering, to that of firms being stakeholders and facilitators of customers' value creation. This means that the firm has to recognise that value creation is essentially conducted and controlled by customers, but the firm has a *role* in helping facilitate it, and the offering is merely a member within the customer's value-creating system. In creating value, customers contribute the resources accessible to themselves to the system to achieve the outcomes in the same way firms deploy resources into offering the product or service. This implies that customers' *abilities* to create value, i.e., using *their* resources, is now *part* of the firm's design and capability space to create value, particularly if it aims to achieve product or service excellence in context. Chesbrough (2011) suggests that customers themselves can take a central role in helping change and shape the firm's offering. This is a change from the traditional 'providing' model where the customer is being passively 'delivered to' or 'served'. The firm's competency to enable value creation in context, and perhaps its potential source of competitive advantage, includes the customer 'as the source of competence' (Prahalad & Ramaswamy, 2000). The firm has to find ways to harness the competency (or improve the lack of competency) of the customer in the value-creating system.

### MINDSET CHANGE 2: VALUE PROPOSITION SITS IN THE CONSTELLATION OF VALUE CREATION

Second, to achieve outcomes within contexts, the customer does not create value with the firm's offerings in isolation. Every context is a 'value constellation' (Normann & Ramírez, 1994) of other firms' offerings playing a role, which means that a more networked approach to the value-creating system is necessary (Demirkan & Goul, 2006). For instance, taking medicine often requires water, and perhaps food to be eaten before or after, sometimes with the help of other products such as syringes or inhalers, and with the aid of other people such as a doctor or a nurse. Every product is therefore an end point of a vertical industry, and it is within the context of use that several vertical industries come together to become members of the individual's value constellation. The firm must therefore make it its business to know the value-creating contexts well and its offering's potential role within them, especially since many of these offerings are interdependent in use-contexts. This capability is inherently a future competitive differentiator, and the move towards acquiring an organisational capability to manage, facilitate and collaborate within the value-creating system is what I call *service transformation* (where I take the term 'service' as an S-D logic view of an offering's competency for value creation). The knowledge and research in this area is embedded in the art and science of service systems (Demirkan et al., 2011).

How do these two mindset changes affect our thinking about value propositions? In the 1980s and 1990s, the term 'value proposition' was coined primarily as the first step towards generating worth. The term was often considered as a form of positioning developed by a marketing department to promote benefits, favourable points of difference or promises of 'received' value when a customer buys an offering from the firm. In some cases, the value proposition was little more than a post-rationalised explanation of what the firm could offer within its current capabilities, constraints and (lack of) imaginative intellect – not least because of the complexities and costs of design changes.

We now have to rethink the term 'value proposition'. Instead of a value proposition that is offered to the customer and then 'delivered' by the firm through an exchange, value proposition has now to be a 'resource proposition' of the firm to fit into the customer's context to create value. In other words, firms can only make a proposition as a potential resource participant in value co-creation. Thus, a company's offering, whether it be goods or services, is merely value unrealised, i.e., a 'store of potential value', until the customer realises it through value creation in context and gains the benefit. Sometimes, customers could also contribute to the value proposition itself. This is what I would term as *co-production*, which is often confused with value creation.

I see co-production as the customer's involvement in the creation of the company's value proposition, e.g., customers helping Samsung design their next smartphone. In contrast, value creation is the customer realisation of the offering to create value-in-context, e.g., *using* the smartphone. Customers are always co-creators of value-in-use contexts as I have described in Chapter 3. Any experience of an offering is already a (co-)creation of value. However, they may not always be co-producers of the firm's offering. In fact, until quite recently, we didn't really co-produce much with firms. With all the crowd-sourcing and open innovation platforms however, engaging customers to co-produce the design of an offering is starting to take off.

Essentially, value creation dictates that both the firm and the customer are active in the creation of value – the former through its value propositions and the latter through its experience of the firm's propositions. Value creation is the enactment and realisation of those propositions, which is why it is also termed as value *co-creation* in some academic literature. Of course, customers choosing to contribute to the firm's offering through co-production also create value for themselves as well, but based on a different proposition from the firm (that of engagement and community perhaps?), and they create a different kind of value from realising that proposition. So co-production could be nested within co-creation value. What this means is that I could derive value from helping the firm design the next version of a tablet PC, which is co-production of the tablet PC's value proposition. While I am doing that, I am co-creating the value of feeling useful and valued but that, of course, is different from the value I create when I *use* that tablet PC.

This view raises a couple of important implications not dealt with by traditional exchange-centric management practices. First, this brings the firm right into the customer value-creating space and time, which would mean that the social, ecological and environmental surroundings, while not possible to be controlled by the firm, become a factor in the firm's design of the offering. Second, the customer's resources to co-create value now

becomes central to realising the firm's value proposition. In other words, what the customer does with the object is of direct concern to the firm, if the firm wishes to be successful.

Thus, through the way we think about value proposition, firms have to think of our bottles of wine, food, desks and shampoo as a bundle of provider resources made available in context when we buy and bring them home for value co-creation towards our outcomes (Vargo & Lusch, 2004; 2008). In the same way, we as customers offer our skill sets and competencies as well as money as our value propositions to the firm so that both sides can come together, first to exchange, and then to create value.

With context as the value-creating system, firms also have to rethink their offerings and business models to understand changing contexts, especially if they integrate digital technologies into their offering. The firm's value proposition is therefore the form in which it believes our needs could be best satisfied across the contexts of our experiences with the product. Since very few individual objects create value on their own, it means a product must consider the boundaries of what it can or cannot do in future contexts.

Since we now have to consider an object or an offering to be part of an experiential use context, rather than be apart from it, it makes us think harder about how we make things in the future, especially if we would like to take advantage of digitisation and connectivity. Objects commonly used or experienced together in context become important. Contexts before and after use also become important as demand for information for the past, present and future becomes central to contexts, especially in terms of how things are used and experienced. Understanding the temporality of contexts creates opportunities for new services to intervene digitally and offer necessary information.

## VALUE PROPOSITION AS AN OUTSOURCED PROPOSITION

Thinking about value propositions in this way is a sharp contrast to the conventional exchange-based world of goods and services. In the exchange-based world, the consumption and experience of services such as insurance, restaurants and travel are far more visible than those for tangible things, and because of the firm's involvement in the experience of services, it is seen to be different from the manufacturing and sale of objects such as fridges, food and furniture.

However, if we think about *why* we buy and the value we create from experience/use, the distinctions between goods and services become less important. In the way we live our lives, we want to achieve certain goals, and our use/experience of offerings occurs because we want to achieve some outcome with them (see Figure 8.1).

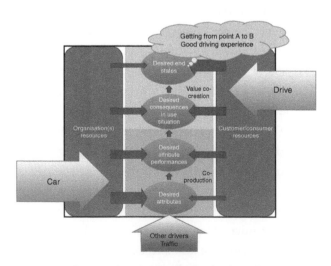

FIGURE 8.1: Symmetric account of value (co-)creation

In some cases such as food, we can only achieve outcomes of being fed and nourished through things. In other cases, achieving a neater and shorter haircut can only be accomplished through buying services. Increasingly, we are able to achieve some outcomes through a choice of things or services, such as getting fit through buying a treadmill or joining a gym.

All offerings, be they things or services, serve lived lives in some way, and the only reason we buy them is because we believe they will make our lives more efficient or effective in achieving our own outcomes. If we stretch that thinking further, we buy because we 'outsource' some things to a product or a service. We could drink water from a tap with our hands but that is not effective, so we buy a cup to hold the water to drink it. By doing so, we have outsourced that function to a cup (Vargo & Lusch, 2011). Just as well, since our hands are not effective in holding coffee anyway.

In this sense, we are all like businesses 'outsourcing' certain functions and activities of our lives to a thing or a service. All goods and services are offerings that make our lives better, through greater efficiency or making us more effective. If we wanted a suit, we could buy the material and make it ourselves or we can commission a tailor to do so. We buy either because we can't do it ourselves, or it's more effective or efficient to have someone else do it and we pay for it. A value proposition can therefore be a service or a thing, but if we think about the outcomes we want, it might be better not to make any distinction but just think about how best we could be served. Traditionally, banking was a service rendered by people but now it is also provided through a mobile phone, becoming more of an object that enables you to serve your own banking needs.

In general, I use the term 'value proposition' to denote some offering that serves us in use/experience that we are willing to buy. I find it easier to think about innovation and new markets when the distinction between a service and a thing disappears. Many traditional services are starting to be offered through digital technologies provided via connected widgets and software. The functionalities of objects are starting to be digitised into cloud-based activities, creating 'services' in homes and offices but also, almost as an incidental by-product, capturing the previously secret clues of that 'private' domain – lifting the lid on how, when and with what they are used.

The boundaries between manufacturing and service are becoming blurred as more goods and services become connected. I would argue that with more 'things' becoming connected and able to serve us in context, everything would be built to be a service in the future, with the firm engaged and involved in individuals' creation of value. Yes, even shampoo! New exchanges based on access are blurring the distinctions further, and traditional markets of ownership exchange are becoming archaic; thinking in that legacy way impedes our ability to be creative and innovative. Traditional value propositions that are based on the production of things or provision of activities to serve customers are beginning to change.

If we consider a value proposition as an 'outsourced' provision that is more efficient or effective to buy rather than to make, then there are degrees to which this type of provision could serve us. Take, for example, getting from the house to town. There are a few options:

(1) walk;
(2) take a bus/taxi;
(3) buy a car;
(4) hire a limousine.

If we wish to get to town quickly or if town is rather far away, walking might be out of the question. A bus or taxi may be a viable option but if we wanted to go into town and also go to other places, buses or taxis may not serve those areas and might also be rather expensive. Buying a car is an option but this would require our own resources and skills (ability to drive) to create value with the car to get the outcome we want.

What I am saying is that when we wish to achieve an outcome, firms have an option to *enable* us to achieve it – selling us a car that has the affordance of drive-ability – or *relieve* us from the activity of having to do it – renting us a limousine to take us to our destination. Every object or service is an 'outsourced' provision that varies in its degree of enabling or relieving us. Note that enabling and relieving are not opposite ends of the same spectrum. Enablement depends on the object or service *affordance to achieve* **outcomes**, while relief depends on the object or service *affordance to relieve* **activities**.

Almost all products that are objects are enabling because we need to employ our own resources and skills to use/experience and create value with them to achieve our outcome. A car is a product that enables us to drive ourselves to many places. A service such as a manicure relieves the individual from tending to her own nails but this service is usually enabled by the facilities and equipment. Thus, every offering is a value proposition that could both enable and relieve the customers to do their part to achieve the outcomes they want. Objects (products), firms' activities (services) and customer practices are therefore components of the total value creation, but the value proposition is the boundary of co-creation beyond which the firm chooses not to participate directly but which the customer would need to perform.

Achieving emotional outcomes such as assurance, status or pride are almost always enabling value propositions. These are derived from products such as a home security system, a luxury handbag or a new car, since no firm can actually relieve customers from their ability to 'feel proud'. Objects can relieve customers from certain decisions though, such as the windscreen rain detector that relieves the driver from deciding when and at what speed to turn on the windscreen wipers. Whether a product is enabling outcomes or relieving activities is also dependent on the outcome and at which level of enablement or relief, since outcomes inevitably lead to other outcomes. A mug may enable us to drink coffee but it relieves us of using our hands to hold the coffee, so a value proposition can be enabling or relieving or both, depending on where we draw the line on the outcome.

Whether a value proposition is enabling customers to co-create outcomes or relieving customers of their activities has a huge impact on the firm's ability to scale its offering, which in turn, impacts on customer choice and variety of use. It is not surprising that enabling value propositions such as products are able to derive scale economies, while relieving value propositions such as services are less able to scale. This is because products can often be more easily standardised and then scaled up when compared to services. Yet, services can accommodate more varieties in terms of the experience/use of the offering. By doing so, customers may be happier and may be willing to pay more, but this makes it harder for the firm to scale up the offering.

If a firm builds a 32-inch TV and customers buy it, the customers can't have it as a 42-inch TV on Saturday when they are hosting a World Cup football party for their friends. However, it does mean that the firm can roll out millions of standard 32-inch TVs for sale, achieving scale economies. This also means that 32-inch TVs can be bought at a much cheaper price since revenues are obtained from a larger market. Conversely, if a firm is handling the catering for the football party at the customer's home, the customer could specify how many tables, chairs, cutlery sets and waiters are required, the arrangement of the marquee and furniture in their garden, and the size of the outdoor projection screen. As a catering firm, personalising and giving choices to customers means that they are probably unable to scale up and serve hundreds or thousands of customers over the same weekend. This scalability constraint means that it would be more expensive to serve each customer.

Digitisation is beginning to change this. How firms can redesign their goods and services to serve their customers in use-contexts is changing, especially with the ability to intervene more directly and serve more effectively through digital technology and connectivity. A good example of this is the smartphone. The smartphone is a scalable object. It is in essence the same object for everyone, and firms like Apple and Samsung can scale its production to make millions of products. Yet, no single smartphone is the same. The market layer of apps accessible via a smartphone allows every individual to personalise and use the smartphone differently at different times. We can find our way to a destination, check train times, use a calculator, compass and see what the weather might be in the afternoon. The smartphone is able to take advantage of the fact that *we* hold the information on when we need a service and when we need certain outcomes. Since we know our own variety of contexts and outcomes in use, we could personalise the service of the phone and make our lives better if we are given the digital ability to do so.

The smartphone also takes advantage of the fact that it is present in almost all our contexts. As an ever-present companion that is carried almost everywhere, its ability to serve us in context is crucial. The smartphone is therefore capable of being standardised and scaled for production, and yet personalised to deal with our many varieties of use in context because it leverages on our resources. It is a tool for co-creation of value at the point of use, but with design boundaries that allow for both personalisation for variety and scalability to occur. In creating the iPhone, Apple has morphed the smartphone into a life-enabling scalable platform for us to improve our abilities in context. The scalability allows Apple to generate millions in revenues, and the ability of the platform to allow cheap apps to be created to assist in lived lives has resulted in an explosion of demand by individuals who have a great need to realise more abilities (through digital services) in context.

It may be worth noting at this point that there is a fundamental distinction between connectivity and content. In the same way that the smartphone is regarded as a generic remote control for our personal digital lives, so the provision of broadband access can be regarded as a standardised generic utility provided entirely independently of the services that run across it. Roads are rarely dedicated to specific traffic types and electricity supplies are, for the most part, provided independently of our individual lighting or heating needs. The teasing apart (and regrouping) of service bundles that may once have seemed committed companions is an important feature of digital innovation.

The future of digitisation, connectivity and new value propositions for firms is therefore a boundary issue as well as a contextual issue.

The *boundary issue* deals with the location of separation between a scalable proposition and high variety of service to allow individuals to personalise their resources in context. In the past, firms would trade off scalability with variety, deciding that there are only certain segments of markets that can be served. This would of course result in limited choices for individuals in terms of creating value-in-context. With new technologies, that trade-off for some attributes may no longer be necessary, and firms seize opportunities both to scale and personalise for use, leveraging customers' information, resources and abilities. Indeed, segmenting may create a competitive *dis*advantage because the firm's competitor may be able to leverage on digital technology to personalise its offering to all.

That 32-inch TV isn't far from being technologically able to become a 42-inch, whenever an individual wishes. The question then becomes whether it is viable to do so. Firms that win are those who understand that variety from contextual experience could be post-purchase and emergent, and yet allow customers to personalise contexts of use with a scalable platform. The scalable platform then allows scale economies which means that customers also benefit from lower prices. It creates a win-win situation where both personalisation for variety and lower prices from scalability can be achieved.

The *contextual issue* deals with how a proposition could serve contexts of use better. The challenge is to envisage how the proposition can be present where customers want it to be at the time they need it. How would a camera, compass or a calculator know when and how we want to use them? The answer did not come from a camera, compass or a calculator but from a phone that is always with us, because these offerings could easily be digitised. A camera manufacturer has recently launched their latest high-end product with an embedded phone! For those objects that are less able to be digitised, the contextual issue will impact on the boundary issue because a value proposition could change its form due to digital technologies. This is why digital technologies could be disruptive, because we could arrive at our outcomes in different ways when we want to use them in context. This is the nature of disruptive or radical business model innovations.

Note that this is not the typical mass customisation issue in manufacturing. Mass customisation traditionally looks at customisation at the point of exchange, customising the offering to what the customer wants to *buy*, rather than how the customer is using it in context.

*Personalisation* for use is different because the customer does not really know their variety of contexts in use often until it happens. Asking the customer to choose/customise at the point of exchange/purchase is essentially just pushing the risk of contextual variety in experience onto the customer, and it is actually poor 'service'. Unfortunately, this is actually commonplace because firms don't understand experiential and usage contexts and are unable to redesign to serve better (see box on retail banking on p. 146).

It is for this reason that the distinction between a product and a service will be irrelevant in the digital economy of the future. Everything industry makes in the future will be a service. Even tea can be a service when you think about when you wish to have tea. If tea companies could find ways of ensuring that the tea you wish to have is available in context (rather than you remembering to get it), getting tea to you becomes a service. Of course, this opens the market to all sorts of intermediaries of different types and the competitive market dynamics that come with it. Firms will shift from being sellers to becoming facilitators of value creation in contexts (Normann, 2001).

---

### Retail banking: a magic wallet

True retail banking service should be a magic wallet for our money. It should be with us all the time in our back pocket or handbag, a convenient wallet that provides quick and secure access to our money whenever and wherever we want it. When we don't need it, it keeps our money safe and gives us interest at the best possible rate. If we don't have enough money, it lends us some at the best possible interest rate. More importantly, it not only gives us these options, it respects us enough to know when to let us choose.

However, retail banking has grown into a monolithic institution, creating rules, transactions, norms, practices that we have come to accept as the 'solution' to our needs, making us jump through hoops in the name of service and security, just to access our money. It has become an institutionalised solution.

Technology, in particular digitisation, can now potentially make this magic wallet come true, e.g., through mobile solutions and other ways to access money. However, institutionalised solutions are hard to de-institutionalise. The current retail banking model is still based on the old goods-dominant logic of exchange, with the belief that revenue (and therefore service) is created at the point of exchange.

Banks try to modify the model to fit by customising their products to give more choices, instead of personalising for our experience. For the consumer however, this results in too many 'choices'. Banks try to use exchange to emulate possible use contexts, but this results in the customer having to make too many choices before the use experience. The value created by retail banking is not at the point of

> **(cont.)**
>
> exchange, but at the point of use in context. My magic wallet creates value with me at the time I need to access, look at and use my money. Making me choose the options for my magic wallet (retail banking solution) before I use is just passing on risks to me. This is just poor service.
>
> With digitisation, banking could actually build contingent revenue models, better context pricing models, i.e., collapsing exchange and use into the same time and space, with new platforms of both exchange and use, better aligning customer outcomes (and needs) to the exchange. Now, that is truly a retail banking service to look forward to.

Yet, there are challenges in understanding how such services could be provided: which types of outcomes they enable or what types of activities they relieve; which aspect of an offering could be scaled; whether all variety of use contexts could be served efficiently and effectively; the form and presence of the value proposition in context, and, to be discussed in the next chapter, how firms derive revenues from this system.

## VALUE PROPOSITION AS AN EMPOWERING PROPOSITION

Value propositions (offerings) are not bought by us just to satisfy an 'outsourced' need. The lessons from the digitisation of photography and new contexts of use for a mobile phone camera come from the fact that such offerings allow individuals to be more efficient and capable at doing what we currently do.

Michael Saylor's book, *The Mobile Wave: How Mobile Intelligence Will Change Everything*, suggests that mobile phones now bestow upon us 'super powers', allowing us to record videos of events as they occur, and potentially influence global politics, as seen by the mobilising effect of social networks used during the 'Arab Spring' of 2011 and beyond. The ability of mobile phones to be omnipresent has turned them into tools for fighting corruption, buying things, improving memory, enhancing education, showing directions and gaining greater access to healthcare. With nearly six billion mobile phones in the world (and 68 per cent of their users claiming that they sleep with them by their beds), the phone is now a platform both for firms to serve us in context and on demand, and to empower us as an instrument of change.

This is an important design consideration arising from contexts of use. Smartphones do not just satisfy a need (to make a phone call, etc.) but their proliferation comes from the fact that, in combination with networked services, they can both take away cognitive effort as well as enable individuals to become better at what we do. This means the firm has to understand when individuals' resources could be used to create value-in-context, and the limit of the firm's ability to create that value.

For example, a mobile phone company may understand that the use of a mobile phone requires some level of quietness, privacy for the conversation and good reception for the call; but it can only provide the reception. The customer, at the point of use, would need to muster contextual – and in some cases material – resources (e.g., going into a room) to achieve end-states at the point of use. In this case, the individual holds greater information and visibility than the firm, resulting in he or she having better access to more contingent resources. A value proposition that enables us to muster those resources better (e.g., telling us where the nearest quiet area is) will make us better at achieving end-states for the value proposition.

Many firms seem to think that a good digital offering in context is one that relieves individuals from making certain decisions. For example, smart meters could relieve us from deciding when the thermostat should be switched on or off, depending on the temperature in the room. However, every relieving decision made by an object would also result in the object not being able to take on contextual variety. For example, I could be suffering from a cold, and would prefer temperatures to be higher on that particular day. An early comedic example is one featured in a short radio story in the 1980s where the central character found, after a long liquid lunch, that he was denied access to his computer on account of an analysis of his speech patterns. Despite his protestations (he claimed that he had a cold), the voice-activated system proceeded to cancel his afternoon meetings automatically, and inform the management that he would be absent and was drunk!

The skill of determining what activities to relieve and what outcomes could be enabled is a challenge in the design and configuration of the contextual service system. The best digital offerings in the world know when to do both. They relieve us of cognitive effort for issues we are concerned about but they also enable us, not merely because of time and space from the relief, but from an expansion of our capability. A smartphone relieves us from remembering our diary but also enables us to organise our family's diaries. Adoption and market penetration are quick if offerings know what activities to relieve and what outcomes can be enabled because this means a person can create more value with less effort.

**Make-it-better or make-me-better**. Taking the concept of affordance in Chapter 4, note that an empowering value proposition falls into two extreme categories; making the value proposition better, or making us better. This is especially relevant for future 'smart' objects.

For example, we could make the house heating system decide when it should warm up and when it should bring temperatures down when we are not home. This is what I call the 'making an object better' mindset (Make-it-Better, MIB). We make the object learn, think, adapt and be smart

so that we don't have to be so. On the other hand, we could take a different approach; Make-me-Better (MMB). We can choose to design an object such that it makes *us* (as human beings) better – designing to affordance – meaning that we design the heating system to *empower us in making better decisions* on when we want the house temperature to be warmer or colder depending on our contextual needs, and leaving the decision to us after giving us the relevant information.

This is an important point for much of experience innovation and engineering design. Research in information systems has discussed concepts of mindfulness and mindlessness in the way we interact with objects, suggesting that there is a tension between them (Carlo et al., 2012). Developing MIB and MMB design parameters goes to the heart of how we think about future smart and connected objects. Should we be making smarter objects or should objects make *us* smarter? Ideally, it should be *both*, but understanding the boundary between an object being a nanny versus an object being a good PA is an important distinction. The MIB approach often creates a function-based closed system and largely ignores the role of the human being, considering human actions that do not behave according to the prescribed behaviour as some variability best ignored or curtailed. The MMB approach creates an affordance-based open system that includes the human being and respects our judgement on deciding what is best for us. The MIB approach creates super objects, while the MMB creates super people, much as the smartphone has enabled us to do and be more.

## VALUE PROPOSITION AS ACHIEVING OUTCOMES

Imagine a value proposition of English language tuition. Traditionally, the contract would include perhaps thirty hours of English tuition, plus textbooks and workbooks. Let's say the entire course would cost £1,000. A teacher contracted to teach this would have a good understanding, not merely of the language, but of the grammar, syntax and all the necessary skills required to teach an English course. That is the traditional model and the teacher's value proposition is in the way the course is taught. Now imagine changing the contract to one where the teacher is judged based on outcomes – payment will be made according to every English word that comes out of the student's mouth in the year following the course (assuming this is measurable).

Contracting on outcomes in this way means that the value co-created with the student includes the student's value proposition – what he or she brings to the context. More importantly, since the teacher is being judged on the outcome of the co-creation, the teacher now has to learn new skill sets – those of motivating the student, building a rapport with the student and getting the student to co-create value – skills that may not usually be part of an English language teacher's traditional skill set. In addition, if the contract has been signed based on a fixed payment made in advance to achieve a certain level of performance, such as a set number of words per month perhaps, then the teacher now has to achieve the outcome at a lower cost. Finally, just to add to the complexity, imagine the student as one who is difficult and culturally different from the teacher.

Figure 8.2 shows a vendor providing an outcome-based service to serve the context of kite flying. The kite vendor fixes up the kite

FIGURE 8.2: Outcome-based kite flying service
Credit: Can Stock Photo Inc./tana

purchased by a little boy and he receives no payment if the kite doesn't fly – which means he needs to fix up a balanced kite to afford flying, teach the boy the skill, and hope for the wind to get the kite aloft. In other words, outcome-based services are designed to include their contexts and constellations.

For many consultants out there, value propositions as outcomes seem to be similar to selling 'solutions'. This is not the case, as there is a fundamental difference between outcomes and solutions.

'Solutioning' means that the product or service is being 'delivered' *to* a passive customer. Achieving outcomes, however, means that the product or service is affording outcomes *with* an active customer. It may not seem much, but these two sets of thinking change the way the firm would think about its offering.

## DIFFERENCES BETWEEN THE DESIGN OF SOLUTIONING AND OUTCOME-BASED VALUE PROPOSITIONS

*A different capability.* The ability of a value proposition to achieve outcomes means the ability to engage with your customer. This is the case for both products and services. In services, it is a capability to co-create, partner and collaborate to attend to customer variety from use contexts. In products, it means the ability to allow the customer to adapt, use and personalise the offering for use contexts. An outcome-based value proposition means you recognise that you need to keep your customers engaged and working with the firm's product or service for the varied benefits they want for themselves, and you develop your product or service capability to allow for that. A solution-based value proposition implies a passive customer. When you deliver 'a solution' it implies the firm can do everything, everything is under the firm's control and the customer stays as a passive 'consumer'.

Companies that don't really know how to collaborate, co-create and partner often prefer solutioning. Why? Because they would like everything under their control. Co-creating and partnering is hard because the firm feels it loses control, and it equates control with scalability and systematic replicability. It does not need to be so. The capability to achieve outcomes is therefore a different capability from solutioning. It's a capability of managing customer autonomy and complexity. Solutioning tells the customer 'I know better', while achieving outcomes tells the customer 'we can both do better'.

*Paradox of solutioning.* The paradox of providing solutions is that the firm relegates the customer to a passive role, therefore making it harder for the firm to please the customer. The logic is that an engaged customer is a happy customer because the firm respects their autonomy and yet is able to manage the cooperation and empowerment. Wanting your customer to be passive is like wanting your child to be passive while you provide everything for the child. This usually doesn't make for happy children.

*Emergent benefits.* Emergent benefits also arise from outcomes and engagement that cannot be 'solutioned'. For example, a firm may be able to provide the 'solution' of constructing a 'village' (build houses, town hall, parks, roads, etc.), but it can never provide a 'community'. That can only be co-created and achieved together. Similarly, many emergent properties of systems such as the notion of 'family' and 'experiences' are co-created and not 'solutioned'. If a customer is outsourcing a service, it needs to be very careful about what outcome it is actually outsourcing. I see customers, especially business customers, specifying functions and tasks to be outsourced and then realising that the culture, ethos and community workplace spirit has disappeared with it. It is easy to think that the world is about tasks and functions. Specifying only the complicated functional outcomes for outsourcing is the most common problem I encounter because it underestimates the full understanding of the 'outsourced' element, and reduces it to a mere function when the original system was achieving more complex outcomes before it was outsourced.

*Variety.* Solutions and reductionistic engineering science in systems are useful when there isn't much variety in the context of customer 'use' of a product or service. Take for example the experience of a flight. In such cases, a fully engineered system could be put in place where almost every contingency has been covered. When you have customers in an enclosed cabin, there really isn't much they would need except to sleep, eat, drink and be entertained. In systems where customer 'use' of a service could have high variety, e.g., a resort hotel, trying to 'command and control' the experience could end up with a rather unhappy customer. Firms need to be careful how they try to limit variety because not only do these firms end up not co-creating value, they engineer a disengaged and indifferent customer. Contextual variety is double-edged. It means more work for the firm but also an opportunity to create better experiences and happier customers. Understanding the firm's role in co-creation and variety also demands a rethink about passive customer satisfaction models that merely assess customers' perception of the provision, but not the value jointly created. The idea of 'satisfaction' is very one-sided. It does not usually assess the customer's own contribution to the co-created value in a service or product.

If we consistently buy goods, commerce will consistently produce them. The move towards outcomes could potentially snowball to have a big impact on sustainability, where quality-of-life improvements (for consumers) and effectiveness and efficiency (for businesses) come not through ownership or consumption of things, but through contracting and buying outcomes. Clearly, such outcomes are delivered not by things alone but by large sets of activities such as supply chains and service systems. And even without passing ownership of goods over to the customer, outcomes are still achieved through resources, albeit different configurations of them. Thus, the convergence of things and activity-based resources for achieving outcomes would result in different resource combinations in a system.

## VALUE PROPOSITION AS PLATFORM

Platforms are increasingly a popular approach in designing value propositions. A platform is a system that can be adaptive with interdependent elements that can each be innovated upon (Gawer &

Cusumano, 2002). It takes a systems approach to value-creating contexts by creating a more structured architecture with a set of rules – the protocols, rights and transaction conditions (Eisenmann et al., 2006). Platforms determine the interfaces between elements and how subsystems work together, even among offerings that are not offered by the firm. These interfaces can allow the firm to innovate on one particular subsystem while another may be in use, as in the case of modular platform architectures (Meyera & DeToreb, 2001).

Financial services often have IT-based platforms on a service-orientated architecture where they can constantly innovate and upgrade their services. Note that a platform for value propositions (i.e., a *market* platform) is not always the same as a platform for various technologies. They could be one and the same – for instance, the iPhone is both a technological platform for apps as software and a market platform for the software as a service value proposition of firms – but they need not be. Firms could have an entire platform as their value proposition serving customers through various sub-services – what economists would call a single-sided market. On the other hand, the platform could be a value proposition of one firm which allows other firms to offer their value propositions on it – a multi-sided market platform. Chapter 10 will discuss the difference between these two platforms.

Firms' platform value propositions are also beginning to include their customers' resources as input to create new value propositions of their own. At the extreme, firms may decide that their customers' resources could be worth more than what they could provide, and that they didn't need to offer anything in exchange except for the space to allow these interactions to occur; take for instance, virtual spaces for sharing photos, music or hobbies. Threadless.com uses 'crowd-sourcing', engaging potential users in the act of designing their own T-shirts. The website runs a weekly competition where anyone can submit a T-shirt design. Through the competition, threadless becomes a multi-sided market enabler to attract a high volume and variety of ideas that become T-shirts for sale.

Platforms are often used because of their ability to modularise themselves for different service propositions. This then allows for them to be configured and reconfigured frequently for deeper personalisation by customers when their contexts change. If a platform moves from a multi-sided to a single-sided market, it is inevitable that many customers' contextual and changing needs will not be served adequately, i.e., the variety will not be attended to and usually, the numbers served will reduce. There have been instances where firms have decided to move back to providing single-sided rather than multi-sided platforms. Myspace was a typical example of how a multi-sided platform for sharing interests in music became a single-sided platform when Newscorp took over. The result is well known; the company that Newscorp bought for US$580m in 2005 was sold for US$35m in 2011.[1]

## NEW BUSINESS MODELS

Business models have been increasingly discussed since the advent of the Internet and the proliferation of e-businesses in the 1990s. We have used terms such as 'Internet business models', 'e-business models' and 'new business models' to compare and show how firms successfully or unsuccessfully conducted their businesses (Osterwalder et al., 2005). Apple's new business model combining 'hardware, software and service' elements has been touted as revolutionary in digital and portable entertainment.

Essentially, a business model is how a firm 'does business'. Both academia and industry have repeatedly discussed how firms could create new business models to compete successfully. I consider a business model as *the way the firm proposes value, creates value and creates worth from the value-creating system* (Osterwalder & Pigneur, 2010). This lines up quite nicely with the three market challenges I highlighted in Chapter 5. Knowing what

---

[1] www.theatlantic.com/technology/archive/2011/01/the-rise-and-fall-of-myspace/69444/. Accessed 1 July 2013

possible forms in which individual needs are fulfilled is the value proposition of the firm. Knowing how these propositions (offerings) become resources is the value creation of the offering with customers, and finally, what can be commodified within the value-creating system that can create worth is the capture of value creation into revenues for the firm. In a sense, the firm's business model is, in a sentence, 'meeting needs, profitably' (which is also the definition of marketing), but in a holistic and systemic way.

The notion of 'new' in new business models suggests that it is not what is current. There are two ways of looking at it. Current business models may be disrupted by other developments or there may be an innovation to create a previously unseen model.

## VALUE CONSTELLATION MAPS AND THEORISING ON DISRUPTIVE BUSINESS MODELS

There are very few proposals on how firms can innovate their business models, especially in the case of radical innovation. Radical business model innovation is a disruption to the firm's core structure and governance, as well as to the way it creates and commodifies the value created in the market. To be able to think through possible disruption requires a mindset shift from the entrenched business model – which is, of course, a challenge when the firm is socialised and embedded within that mindset.

One way of doing this is to create a *value constellation map* by examining closely the different industries involved in a particular use/experiential context, in terms of their value propositions. A value constellation map is a map of all the entities within contextual archetypes i.e., the *nouns* within the value-creating system.

Let me illustrate this with one particular context and its value constellation map. Consider the case of Emily, who is listening to music on Spotify premium, a music-sharing service, while at the gym (see Figure 8.3). She sees her friend Sarah listening to a track from a group they both like and decides to listen to that track as well.

FIGURE 8.3: Enjoying music in the gym, sharing music with others Credit: Can Stock Photo Inc./ 4774344sean

In between sessions on different gym equipment, Emily and Sarah chat briefly on Facebook messenger service.

We analyse the context from the perspective of Emily. Within Emily's context are elements – music, smartphone, earphones, air-conditioning, gym equipment. There are also elements that Emily needs but may not be so obvious such as the facilities within which the gym is located. Within Emily's context, she creates value with music, smartphone, Facebook, gym and connectivity service through her practices – exercising, listening, typing, sharing. She creates meaning and value (goodness) from the interactions between the elements and herself. There are rules within the context – such as how Emily goes about those practices and appropriate behaviours within that context. Within Emily's value-creating system are firms that propose value to her through the offerings in context.

We can therefore identify the members in the constellation based on each of their value propositions in context. Connectivity is provided through the broadband provider in the gym, or perhaps 3G through a telco. Music content is provided through a licensee, e.g., EMI. The smartphone is a value proposed by Apple or Samsung, the equipment and exercising activities are values proposed by the gym and the social platform is the value proposed by Facebook (see Figures 8.4 and 8.5).

Formulating a value constellation map allows us to see the business models of all stakeholders that have a role within this value-creating context. This could help us identify where disruption could happen because we can identify which industry has a stake in

E.G. MUSIC – CONTENT

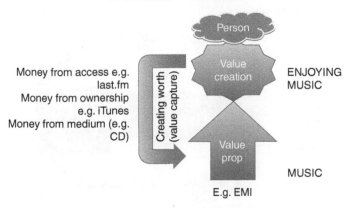

FIGURE 8.4: Business model of music licensee

E.G. MUSIC – CONNECTIVITY

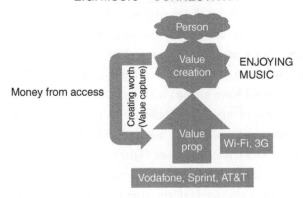

FIGURE 8.5: Business model of connectivity business

the value-creating context. When we understand that, we can then create scenarios of design for each value proposition to see how one value proposition could converge with another, or how one firm could encroach on another firm's territory. This could be done as an ideation or brainstorming group but in a systematic manner.

By understanding value creation in context and creating a value constellation map in this way, we can create a methodology for innovation, particularly disruptive innovation. A few extensions from such a methodology could help build better scenarios. For example, we could

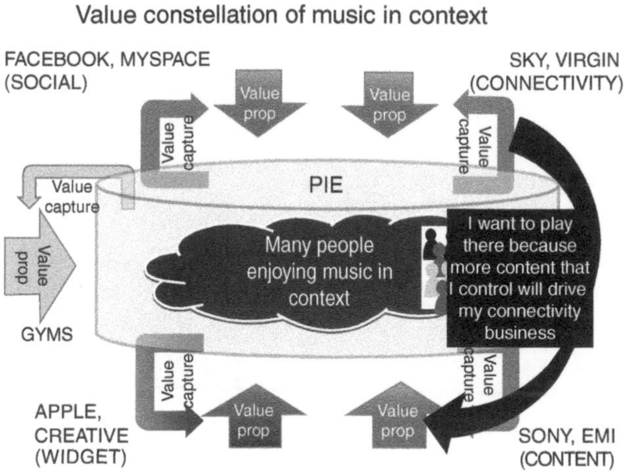

Value constellation of music in context

FIGURE 8.6: Industry verticals in the value-creating context

go back to the section on the emergence of latent needs, and consider *the contextual demand for information* and the response from the value propositions in context. Before Emily came to the gym, was there some information she could get about how crowded it was, or whether she could have a word with her trainer? If she wanted some information, where and how could it be provided by the different sources of services rendered to her by connectivity, the widget, the content or the social platform? (see Figures 8.6 and 8.7) While Emily is at the gym, is she concerned about what she needs to do after her workout, and does she need information for where she is going to next?

We could also use the value constellation map to investigate *context catalysts* for resources. For example, what are the most common stresses to Emily in the gym, or what could make Emily's gym experience better? Perhaps she usually forgets her bottle of water or towel. If this is the case, how could elements (value propositions) within the context assist in serving her in context? What does Emily do if she gets a sudden call or a message that might disrupt her gym time? How can the elements help?

Finally, what other *varieties of experience* could emerge in such a context? For example, how do different people experience the gym

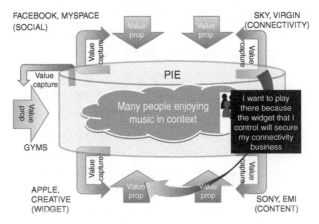

FIGURE 8.7: Industry verticals and contextual competition

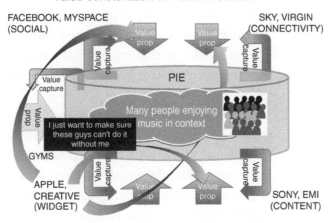

FIGURE 8.8: Industry verticals and contextual competition

differently? Could there be other configurations of the elements proposing value-in-context for them in different ways (see Figure 8.8)?

These are ways to tease out latent needs within the context and to create scenarios so that each firm's value proposition within the constellation could respond in order to provide a solution to those latent needs. Applying earlier lessons on latent needs and solutions in value creation, we could also use *effectual reasoning* and do a *time/space map on the modularity of the context* to see what possible solutions could emerge from the incumbent elements within the context. By thinking through the context systematically, we can generate ideas and scenarios on changes to value creation and the firm's value propositions in context in response to changes. This method could also help to de-institutionalise mindsets and liberate creativity in the design of future products. Plausible scenarios and products can then be worked on in terms of changes to their business models and looking at ways of creating worth. This will be covered in the next chapter.

Aside from generating opportunities from contexts, we could also generate scenarios of threats to each industry. When or how would one industry vertical be threatened by another? Some scenarios on the dynamics between the different industries at play and possible encroachment of one into the other from Emily's context are depicted in the earlier figures. They show why one particular stakeholder could be interested in entering another's territory, and therefore allow us to understand when and why disruption could happen.

This is already rearing its head. On 8 October 2012, Google launched their credit card for small businesses that can be used towards buying Google's advertising. With small businesses not being able to get credit, advertising expenditure suffers. This means Google has a stake in small businesses' ability to raise cash. By issuing credit cards with very generous payment terms, Google is in effect taking over the banks' role, and in so doing, safeguarding their own revenues from advertising.

As more activities become digitally visible and more technologies are able to measure what could not be measured before, connectivity and cloud-based services will bring greater visibility to value-creating contexts and show up contextual neighbours within the constellation which could result in more disruptions. For example, if the supermarket has the biggest stake in your car due to your grocery shopping, they could be willing to subsidise your car insurance or fuel if you are willing to allow your car location and driving capability to be digitally visible. Telematics insurance is already available

for those of us who do not mind showing that we are safe drivers by allowing sensors to be installed in our cars and therefore deserve lower insurance premiums.

Radical and disruptive business model innovation is just beginning with new digital technologies. This means that innovating on a value proposition in the future truly depends on how well the firm understands the context in which their customers realise their value propositions, *especially in conjunction with other value propositions within the value-creating system and other possible services they might require in such contexts.* This means that the membership of an offering in the number of value constellations becomes crucial for understanding the future of disruptive and radical innovations.

Value constellations are a map of 'nouns', which sit within contextual archetypes of rules, verbs, time and space. New configurations will emerge when firms change their offerings' affordance (innovate) for customers' agency to achieve their outcomes. The battle for context is when each offering wishes to redraw its boundary for value creation, encroaching other offerings, usually because one industry feels threatened by bottlenecks or stresses in the contextual system. Since the revised boundary could potentially increase demand, or safeguard markets and prices, it is natural to assume that firms will venture beyond their normal territories. Wessel and Christensen (2012) suggest that firms could prepare themselves from being disrupted by:

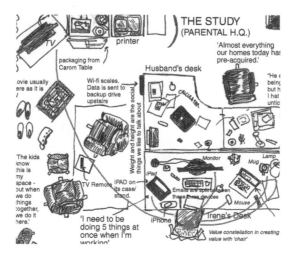

FIGURE 8.9: A value constellation map of my chair

- identifying the strengths of the disrupter's business model;
- identifying the firm's relative advantages; and
- evaluating the conditions that could help or impede the disrupter from appropriating your current advantages.

A value constellation map has been created as a layer on the dialecta-gram of my lived life (see Figure 8.9 which is a section of the full map; courtesy of the EPSRC SeRTES project) to illustrate the value constellation of a chair when I create value with it in my study. From this value constellation map, the chair has a stake in my mug. While I don't think a mug incorporated into my chair is viable, it serves to illustrate a way of thinking about disruptive innovation.

We are used to seeing the 'verticals' of industry and firms derive revenues from such verticals. For example, the purchase and use of a simple object such as a razor is at the end of a long chain of a vertical industry, starting from materials to manufacture to eventual use by us. Similarly, every object you see in Figure 8.9 is the end of a vertical industry. In the case of the razor, it means that *someone*, whether the wholesaler, distributor, retailer, manufacturer or you – has paid for this razor. There are many models within the verticals of course, but essentially, we are used to thinking about value chains as ways to distribute revenues and costs.

Future digital connectivity will disrupt this way of thinking. If vertical industries all sit together within the contexts of use, then there is no stopping one vertical from 'monetising' or commodifying worth within the context of value creation they are participating in. In other words, if a vertical industry is a member of a value constellation, that industry could derive some of the revenues from some other vertical, *through* the horizontal value-creating context, by taking advantage of these lateral dependencies created through such contexts. Such *systemic* business models, evidenced by Google, are already coming into play and will become more commonplace in the future. With digital connectivity, value constellations can even transcend physical time and space, reaching out across multiple geographical constellations and dipping into the revenue streams of other verticals. This means that digital connectivity will spur greater lateral dependencies across such physical times and spaces to create future disruptive effects. The next chapter will expand on this.

Competitive advantage would go to firms that have the greatest understanding and visibility of such value-creating contexts, and are able to strategise on how their customers could be better served, hopefully before their contextual neighbours decide to play in the same space. It also implies that every company, whether digital or not, will be a digital company in the future. If a firm thinks that its offering could never be influenced by technology and digital connectivity, it might want to watch its back, because a competitor could be surging ahead of the game or worse, the firm may be disrupted horizontally by a completely different player.

## CHAPTER 8 REFLECTIONS

We understood from the previous chapter that the *co-creation* of value with intense customer contextual engagement is the cornerstone of future markets – and we should also be clear that this is quite different from *co-production*, where customers are engaged in the design process of an offering.

From the firm's perspective, the enablement of co-creation has at least two creatively disruptive impacts. It signals the end of a mindset that has a sale at the end of the line and demands that they see beyond the buffers to being a stakeholder and facilitator in value creation. Moreover, it also demands that the firm's ability to provide anything in this new market includes the customer 'as a source of competence'.

Nor should they ask 'for whom the bell tolls', for every firm's offering is a member of the value constellation of another firm's value-creating system. So the old familiar boundaries are changed and researchers everywhere see massive disruption as, for example, supermarkets gain expertise in diet-linked e-health, well-being and the promotion of cookery skills. It may do 'exactly what it says on the tin' but the 'doing' is done by the customers and the outcomes, the value creation hinges on their contextual abilities, other products (clean brushes?), the environment, and so on.

This is outsourcing on a scale not previously understood, and the boundaries – the old demarcations – become blurred and irrelevant. We think of this as a challenge for firms but it's as much a challenge for the great silos of state (the departmental responsibilities of government ministers), and – hands up – do I see anyone who has never wished for joined-up policy?

With every product now needing to be aligned in some way to a service, the new value propositions are largely about empowerment – allowing or enabling an individual to do a better job of making use, a better job of creating value. So we either make the thing better, we make customers better or we do both. The widespread enablement of this empowerment does of course depend on the adequacy and availability of platforms – the smart mobile phones, the sensors, the future-proofed connectivity that remove those last-generation constraints on value co-creation.

The business model implications of all this are profound. Only by understanding value creation in context and creating a value constellation map can we develop a methodology for innovation and particularly *disruptive* innovation. These notions may be scary and the impacts uncertain. Hindsight will reveal the wisdom of our choices and the gaps in our understanding of the true role of digital infrastructure.

# 9  Creating viability and worth

For value propositions to create new markets, they must, in some way, be compensated. Many firms forget that it is the market that makes offerings viable and not the single customer. Let me explain.

## COMMERCIAL VIABILITY

I have often been asked to address the challenge of increasing customers' willingness to pay. One company told me that their device and technology was becoming increasingly expensive and customers were not willing to pay more. This 'cost-based' mindset is not helpful because if we think about many things in life, it is hardly a single individual that pays for the cost of provisioning an offering. It is the total market that delivers sufficient revenues to make it viable to serve the entire market.

We pay only 69 pence for apps and, say, £15 a month for 3G infrastructure on our phone, not because that's how much it cost the firms to provide them, but because these offerings are able to be scaled up to serve millions, thus requiring the individual to pay only very little. Instead of asking the question of whether the customer is willing to pay more, it is more helpful to think about how we could make customers pay less, which means scaling an offering to reach wider markets. This is one of the reasons that ubiquitous cloud computing services are soaring in sales, with worldwide figures expected to triple in number to nearly US$73 billion by 2015. Where previously a client needed to install and maintain both hardware and software of information systems (expensive and not easily scaled), cloud providers are able to offer thousands of businesses the same software services at a fraction of the cost because providers have found cloud computing to be a scalable proposition to serve thousands of businesses. In short, the lesson to learn is not how much the customer is willing to pay, but the firm's ability to scale to such a degree that customers do not have to increase their willingness to pay, because the firm is able to sell to many more of them.

If an offering is not commercially viable, it would not be introduced into the market at all. Commercial viability for an innovative offering therefore has two major components: total revenues and total costs. Note that costs do not mean those of producing the offering alone. They also include the cost of accessing and reaching the context through which the offering could be exchanged and served. Similarly, total revenues don't just mean revenues from the offering, but also how much revenue the firm can generate from the customer value-creating context which may not just be from the offering, but also from its tangential services and products within the constellation that could achieve an ideal context for value creation. For instance, top restaurants recognise that parking space may be scarce, and they offer valet parking service so that patrons do not need to face the hassle of looking for a car park.

Looking at total costs and total revenues in aggregate and not attributing them to individuals also means that the viability of a value proposition comes almost entirely from whether the total revenues received would be higher than the total costs of the offering. Even when we say that some markets are difficult to serve and firms have no access or face difficulty with access, it is still a market issue. It just means that the costs for access are so prohibitively high that customers are not willing to pay for the offering. Where costs could be extremely high but customers are willing to pay, it could still be viable. Space travel, for example, may serve only very few. Yet for the few willing to pay, it can be viable. This is why many military equipment productions are still viable, even if they only have one customer. On the flip side, even when many customers are willing to pay, the firm may still find the costs of serving them too expensive, perhaps because they all want the offering served differently. For example, it is often accepted in logistics that the 'last mile' of getting a package to a customer accounts for 80 per cent of the delivery costs. If customers are too costly to serve because the market exhibits too high a variety, a value proposition quickly becomes unviable, especially when these customers are unwilling to pay for being different from the rest.

What the above implies is that the costs of serving the market are not merely recoverable from one or a few customers but from the entire market, whether the market is one or one million. More customers mean that revenues increase not from each individual's willingness to pay, but by the scale of market aggregation. This is the typical characteristic of a one-sided market, and the key to a one-sided market is that there are two players within it – the market and the firm. The optimal solution is to increase viability from *both* revenue increase and cost reduction.

Firms also often assess viability as though revenues are the direct consequence of the costs of the offering. In the first part of this book, I mentioned that we are now seeing more cases where the creation of worth is not the same as participating in the creation of value. This means that a firm could contribute to value creation as a proposition, but may not be compensated directly for that proposition. This is the principal reason why, in this book, I separate the creation of value from the creation of worth.

This fragmentation of the traditional 'value chain' goes to the heart of how we think about 'production'. We have been conditioned to think that whatever firms put their resources into should generate a return that is higher than the costs they have sunk.

As a consequence, many firms still think of the price of their offerings as 'cost-plus', ignoring the value the customer creates with the offering and the context in which value creation occurs.

Value chain thinking came from Michael Porter's 1985 book *Competitive Advantage*, where he proposes the value chain as a chain of activities that a firm operating in an industry performs so as to 'deliver' something that is of monetary value. Thus, many 'business units' are formed in industry to put into operation the ideas around the construction of a value chain. In traditional ways of thinking, products pass through a chain of activities sequentially, and at each stage the product gains some 'value' or in my terms, worth. This sequential chain of activities should then 'add' more worth than the sum of the cost of the activities.

The value chain model clearly doesn't work well when compensation for an offering isn't through ownership. The worth created may instead be the offering's *role* in value creation. For example, a value proposition to achieve outcomes for the customer would not follow any 'chain' at all because multiple entities not within the control of the firm result in the outcome, e.g., being paid only when equipment is being used, which would depend on the customer's need (Ng et al., 2013), other related equipment or supplies. The notion of value chain proliferated the idea that if a firm wanted to make money, revenues would come from a party in the value chain. For example, when a computer is manufactured, this would need to be paid for by the manufacturer, the wholesaler, the distributor, the retailer or the customer, and often every party in the channel (because they 'add value' which means adding worth) gets compensated by customer revenues. As a result of this mindset, we often only think about revenue streams as those which come from the vertical channel.

If we take the lessons from this book however, every vertical channel culminates in a horizontal or systemic context of use. This means that when an offering creates value with a customer, the verticals have access to other verticals within the context of use, and the use context exhibits horizontal dependencies between them. This implies that revenues could be derived from other verticals or within the system because they are members of the same value constellation. For example, it is not hard to imagine that we could pay for broadband at home through some margin taken from our purchases online. Retailers have done this for years. We do not pay for retail experiences at Harrods or Bloomingdale's because this is built into the price of our shopping items. While this is commonplace at markets that are in stores or online, markets of the future will be formed much closer to our lived lives and could exist on smartphones, smart homes, etc. Chapter 10 will discuss this further.

Within the decade following the appetite for aggressive (and largely independent) competitive advantage emphasising the vertical, the notion of *collaborative advantage* is emerging – reflecting the growing awareness (prompted by a gradual appreciation of greater connectedness) of the limitations of stand-alone 'vertical' propositions. Even when many vertical value propositions are still a transfer of ownership, firms are beginning to think about their role in creating value-in-context, in part because of competitive pressure and in part for considering business models of the future. In such cases, applying an S-D logic may be more useful for innovation and future designs.

## THE CHANGING LANDSCAPE OF MANUFACTURING AND SERVICE

Under S-D logic, manufacturing business models will change as objects and services merge through the use of pervasive digital technologies (Ng et al., 2013). For the past century, manufacturing has been essential to wealth creation but many developed economies are gradually becoming service economies. In the case of equipment manufacturers, many have diversified into service provisions to remain viable, aiming to facilitate use of the equipment for customer outcomes rather than just transferring the ownership of equipment. This means that the value proposition of the manufacturer changes from creating worth through the transfer of equipment ownership, to creating worth by achieving outcomes of equipment in use. As I have mentioned previously, outcome-based value propositions such as Rolls-Royce's 'Power-by-the-hour®' exemplifies such a change in value proposition.

When a manufacturer creates worth from achieving outcomes rather than transfer of ownership, it has to deal with (1) the role of the product; (2) the role of the service and (3) the role of the customer (Ng & Briscoe, 2012). The product delivers a performance – e.g., power from an engine. Since mechanical things will always break down, the service will provide uninterrupted operation such as ensuring that backup engine and spares are on hand – e.g., supply chain, repair and maintenance. Finally, since continual use of equipment sits within the customer's space, the customer's resources (and cooperation) have to be managed to achieve use for their own outcomes (Ng et al., 2010). These outcomes could be required in highly diverse environments – e.g., flying in sandy conditions or through ash clouds.

This could suggest that the value proposition for outcomes may be unscalable, but some of my research in this area has shown that it can be scaled if the firm considers where the boundary is between the product and the service and more importantly, where the boundary is between the firm's value proposition (product and service) and customers' value-creating activities to achieve the outcomes. The optimal boundary is to leverage on customer activities and the firm's service activities to deal with varieties of contextual use and experience, but create a platform that is absolutely scalable. Get the boundary wrong and an offering could be unscalable. Many have claimed that service activities are unscalable because they are often human in nature, but the real reason for scale barriers could be the product itself. If the product is designed and manufactured such that the service activities and the customer activities cannot be easily repeated or managed, it may not be the fault of the service or the customer but that of the product around which the services and customer are interacting. This often happens when the product has been manufactured according to the traditional value proposition, i.e., for transfer of ownership, rather than for use or experience. Many manufacturers have told me that if they were going to make a product and obtain revenues through the life of its use, they would not have designed or made it that way (Ng & Briscoe, 2012).

Many successful firms are beginning to recognise the competitive advantage of creating markets for use. For example, Dulux paint produced by Akzo Nobel (formerly Imperial Chemical Industries) is able to create almost any colour a customer wishes through a paint-mixing service (often provided by retailers and decorators). Yet, their proposition is hugely scalable because they manufacture large quantities of core paint colours that, when mixed, can create many different permutations. It leaves customers to decide what colour they wish to have, the retail service to mix paints for the customers and the factory to create scale economies from core paint colours. Yet, even within the core paint colours, there is some variety such as indoor or outdoor paint, types of surfaces, or type of finish. Dulux combines manufacturing for scalability with end-user deep personalisation achieved through the customer's own resources and service provision. In doing so, it is able to achieve high variety and high scalability. The final step of being paid through each square metre of painted surface is perhaps not far off, especially when nanotechnologies can be embedded into paint such that the paint becomes a sensor when it is coated onto surfaces.

All this is set to change even more for manufacturers, especially with *additive manufacturing*, more commonly known as 3D printing. This is a process of making three-dimensional solid objects from a digital model using additive processes, where an object is created by laying down successive layers of material. 3D printing is usually conducted through a materials printer using digital technology, and while per unit prices are more expensive than mass production, 3D printing's ability to produce at low quantities makes it more viable for some manufacturers. It is used in the making of jewellery, footwear, industrial design, prototypes of models in automotive, aerospace, and even for objects to be used by the dental and medical industries.

3D printing can potentially revolutionise traditional manufacturing, further pushing the boundary between what is scalable and what serves the local customer variety. For example, part of a product could be scaled up to produce millions of items while another part of a product could be made using 3D printing to serve the variety the customer wishes to have. Think about how this could transform our factories worldwide – where parts of products that are scalable could be made in low-cost regions of the world and the product finished off at local economies to suit varied conditions of use and experience. The implications for wealth and job creation are profound. Combine this ability with digital connectivity at the customer's use end, and manufacturing in ten years' time could look very different. This example of a digital backwash as I have previously mentioned, is also making us think about converging devices and things in different ways. As manufacturers start to think about scaling their technical core platform, mono-usage products can now become modularised offerings. Imagine manufacturing a 'base' platform on top of which a light, a humidifier or a kettle could be placed. The 'iPhone' of manufacturing is yet to come.

How then should the firm think about scaling and serving highly diverse markets of use? This is a big question that has been neglected in much of research. This is because it involves the interaction between operations management, manufacturing and engineering on the scalability part, and economics, marketing and social sciences on the service, variety and diversity part. It has also been neglected because the view of value has been the same as worth, both of which are seen as resulting from exchange. If we take value as created in experience, and worth as created from some way of generating revenues from that contextual experience, it is clear that our current academic disciplines and the way researchers have been compartmentalised are inadequate to address this issue. In their effort to survive and remain viable, firms will probably restructure their functions more speedily, but may not know what alternative management structures could be feasible in this new digital world. Nonetheless, institutionalised rules from a few hundred years of an industrial era have created path dependencies within each research discipline and business function that makes the reorganisation of firms, and that of academia, challenging.

## REVENUE MODELS FOR CREATING WORTH FROM VALUE CREATION

Traditionally, firms create worth by making something or offering an activity. Customers assess that worth and pay for it. They then create value with it in its use and experience. Digital connectivity is changing this model. We can now see that the firm's value proposition for value creation (what it 'offers') and its creation of worth (how it acquires revenues), although related, may no longer be so straightforward. That means that the value proposition that is potentially a resource for the individual to create value may not be the reason for the compensation or payment. The compensation could come from other sources within the value-creating context.

In the case of Facebook, it has created a social network platform for use by a billion individuals, but the economic compensation does not come from its value proposition. Instead it comes from the hope that you would click on advertisements on its web pages. Some online game sites do not require that customers pay to play, but to compensate the gaming firm by buying some virtual 'goods'. According to some reports, about 48 per cent of the online gaming population said they had purchased in-game currency during 2010, while 47 per cent had bought maps and new levels, and around 29 per cent had purchased armour and equipment.

How then, should firms be thinking of creating worth? The key issue for creating worth is that the firm must have *a role* in value creation. Membership in the context of value creation gives access to the firm to create worth from disrupting other verticals or from within the horizontal, i.e., to derive revenues from that context. This role can be executed in a few ways. If we return to Chapter 4, the contextual experience of value creation has been systematically laid out.

The firm's traditional role is to propose value through one of the elements, e.g., if I am watching TV, the firm could have sold me the TV, or if I was surfing the Internet, the firm could be charging me for connectivity. From understanding business model disruption in Chapter 8, we see that this does not need to be the case. Google does not charge for its search engine; eBay does not charge you to enter its marketplace to buy – it charges sellers. The firm's role in the context of value creation could be any of the components of value creation. In other words, instead of charging the individual for the value proposition itself (the object), the firm could charge for the platform (the value-creating context), other elements in context (contextual neighbours), the practices (verbs) and structure/governance within the context (rules), or facilitate the customer's ability to create value (agency), or charge for outcomes.

The important aspect of value creation is to be in the game, and the firm has to be present in that context to play a role. Each proposal can now be considered.

**Platform revenues**. Charging customers and other firms to access and use a platform is a common revenue model for some online gaming companies. Access to the World of Warcraft, a massively multi-player online role-playing game (MMORPG), requires a subscription fee. Most platform operators try to entice membership through a freemium model (i.e., get the basic service free, upgrade to fee-paying for a premium service; Teece, 2010) or having one party subsidise the other such as PayPal charging vendors only. Such a revenue model makes it easy to establish a large customer base, but the conversion of free users into paying customers is challenging for firms.

Economics literature on platform revenues (i.e., two-sided markets) have discussed a number of market characteristics that play an important role in determining whether the platform firm can profit when members interact on it. It also investigates whether a dominant platform will tend to emerge. These studies suggest that a range of pricing options are available to platform firms: are they only able to charge simple prices, or can they continue to subsidise one side of the transaction or use contracts with payments contingent on continued participation and interaction levels? Would platform members 'multi-home' or could they be constrained to the firm's platform? Can the platform firm monitor or regulate transactions between members? Basic pricing principles discussed in literature have added to our understanding of how and when platforms are likely to survive and why.

Platform revenues are derived from having a value proposition that controls the platform and (ideally) facilitates value creation. In a non-digital world, this could be theme parks or public spaces. Often, such platforms are provided by public services, as private companies may not be willing to invest in the infrastructure. Note that there are two types of platforms. First, *exchange platforms* such as eBay or Amazon facilitate multi-sided markets for the buying and selling of products and services. Second, *experience platforms* such as Facebook, games platforms or public parks facilitate interactions and value creation of objects and people.

Exchange platforms serve the exchange of money and value propositions – the potential of value creation, as I have mentioned in Chapters 4 and 5. Experience platforms serve value creation and interactions – i.e., the kinetic. As an illustration of the difference between the two, many retailers have exchange platforms where they sell their merchandise to customers. In fashion retailing, big brands such as Zara and Topshop have apps for purchasing their clothes. The focus of these big brands has obviously been on selling (worth) rather than value creation, which is the use and experience of the clothes.

Since the advent of digital technologies, new digital offerings that help in value creation have entered the market. Wardrobe Assistant is an app for organising clothes, through which we can match, create looks and keep track of all our clothes in our wardrobe – useful especially when we have very little wardrobe space! Yet, we see fashion retailers not at all interested in the experience of clothes or in the membership of other objects within the value constellation of clothes experience such as jewellery, cosmetics, etc.

With fashion retailers still fixated on exchange and not serving customers in context as part of their full fashion experience, their markets are vulnerable to disruption. The greater the separation between selling and using, and the less a firm cares about the experience of an object versus its purchase, or about the other members within the experiential value constellation, the more vulnerable the firm is to disruptive technologies. Where it has been possible for purchase and usage channels to collapse into the same time and space, demand expands, competitive advantage is created and an increase in revenues usually follows.

Some firms such as Spotify and Deezer are already moving into a combined space of exchange and experience. They allow the platform to interact with others and create value in experience as well as in buying and selling. These platforms often offer fully digital products (such as music) which can create exchanges very close to contexts of use. These platforms have the biggest potential for digital offerings of the future as they can serve both the potential and the kinetic. When this happens, latent needs that surface in context (the kinetic) can be fulfilled on demand (buying the potential) and experienced immediately. Facebook's biggest challenge is that it is a 'kinetic' platform, i.e., it is a platform for interactions, value creation and socialisation. Unless it rigorously makes us buy, it is not a platform to tap into our potential latent needs. More importantly, it is often used on a computer which is a rather flat, two-dimensional interface for looking and clicking that takes us away from our day-to-day lived lives and therefore does not allow a manifestation of our latent needs. It will be interesting as Facebook moves into the mobile space to see how the platform will evolve and if it can create worth from both the kinetic and the potential, in the real time and spaces of lived lives.

All platforms provide access to players to create new revenues from the interactions and even to disrupt other vertical offerings who are members of the same platform. Industry dynamics play a big role in the creation of such platforms. Money is a commodity that is most easily digitised and indeed, much of its use already is. Yet, the use and experiences of money have very few platforms except perhaps for PayPal and M-Pesa. This is because money is a sensitive issue for most people and it exists within a heavily regulated industry. Lumbered with the baggage of regulation, security and sensitivities, innovation has been slow. As a consequence, the many ways in which we would like to use money may not be served adequately. Clearly within Africa, where Western-style bank accounts are not endemic, the use of innovative mobile platforms for transactions (such as M-Pesa) is far more advanced than the European experience. The regulatory inhibitions in African countries seem to have been safely addressed, and M-Pesa has now launched a similar service in India. Challenges faced by the operator, however, have illustrated that moving into this type of service demands a higher order of design and investment commitment with a longer development path relative to traditional product enhancements for mobile services.

**Strategic elements – revenues from gatekeeping**. In Chapter 4, I proposed that value creation exists within a system of not just one value proposition but others as well. Worth can therefore be created from plugging the gaps and understanding the contextual neighbours that an individual might need in order to create value with other objects. As an illustration, food courts are an example of platforms that are both kinetic and potential (you buy food from different sellers within the food court, then you sit down at a table to eat). However, many food courts retain the sale of beverage as part of the platform because getting drinks is an essential element within the system. By providing different kinds of drinks to supplement your food, the platform is able to facilitate your enjoyment of the food court. Offering beverages in a food court is also a strategic element to value creation because it could impede or facilitate value creation through its provision. Outsourcing this to a third party may not be in the interest of the platform provider.

In the same way, Apple's decision to introduce Apple Maps instead of allowing iPhone users to continue utilising Google Maps was aimed at controlling strategic elements of value creation within the mobile platform for future creation of worth. While individuals do not pay for Apple Maps per se, they have already paid for the platform of the phone which includes strategic apps, and these elements will be the gatekeepers for ensuring that value creation continues to be facilitated in the future for the platform. The strategy backfired since Apple Maps was a poor alternative to Google Maps, and Apple had to climb down from its decision and reinstate the latter on its iPhones a few months later.

These strategic elements will also dictate worth creation by generating the *conditions* for accessing the platform in the future. Conditional access is big business today. It is the protection of content where certain criteria need to be met before the customer is granted access to a set of content. The term is commonly used in digital TV systems, especially satellite TV. NDS, a global company with conditional access scrambling and encryption technology used in many of our set top boxes for satellite TV (e.g., TiVO, Sky, Virgin), ensures that non-subscribers cannot have access to TV content to which they have not subscribed. The company was acquired by Cisco in March 2012. In the digital economy where many platforms are increasingly created to facilitate contextual value creation, gatekeeping holds the key to creating worth by deciding who gets access to whom and what.

**Systemic and structural (rules and practices) revenues**. In Chapter 4, I explained how value is created in context through the system of practices and the structures that are in place for these practices. Value creation is therefore enacted through practices and with these come a set of rules. Social rules are those which we tacitly enact, e.g., using a napkin or not talking with

your mouth full, and some are imposed by platform owners. For example, if we take the home as a platform, some households have rules that all members clear their plates and put them into the dishwasher after they have finished dinner, and leave their shoes at the door.

For every rule that demands contextual conformance, there is the potential to create worth from *not* conforming to it. Rules are often put in place so that the context could be better managed, repeated and scaled, and variety could be reduced. Yet, there are revenue models that allow individuals to pay more not to conform. For example, applying for a visa extension in the UK is usually a cumbersome exercise with much documentation to submit and rules to follow. One is charged around £1,500 for applying by post and £1,800 for applying in person. However, for a super premium service of an additional £6,000, a courier will collect application forms and documentation, with officers visiting the applicant to capture biometric information (fingerprints and facial photograph) and obtain his or her signature; a decision will then be made on the application within twenty-four hours of receiving the biometric information.

Contexts where value is created, in homes, offices, digital spaces, etc., will always have structures that dictate rules, and sometimes these are a subset of a general norm. These rules dictate the practices of value creation. Revenues can often be attained from variety and degree of conformity to the rules. By doing so, individuals' value-creating practices (the verbs) can change, and worth can be created from allowing that flexibility. In France, 70 per cent of music played on the radio between 8am and 8pm must be by French artistes. Could there not be an option for radio stations to reduce that percentage and pay to do so? Instead of saying that something cannot be done because it is out of a norm or a rule, there might be a case for increasing price or worth for someone who would like to do things differently. The marginal revenue received from those who want the rules to be different may be higher than the revenues from those abiding by the norm. This may mean that those conforming to rules could benefit from giving flexibility to those who might want it.

It also means that the compensation may not just be monetary, but could also be in other forms. For example, where the public is not allowed to dip into public fountains or draw graffiti on public walls, they could be allowed to do so on one day in the year for stimulating play and creativity. Of course, this calls to question the fairness of such a mixed system but the point I am making is not to regulate one set of stakeholders, but to provide choice based on compensation to personalise for all stakeholders. This is not because we want the compensation or revenue, but because it creates the right sort of behaviours and makes more people happy because choices and freedoms have been considered.

**Revenues from agency and individual skills.** When value creators do not have sufficient agency, value creation is hindered. A person who does not know how to use an oven or play with the Wii cannot create any value with it. Agency is therefore a part of a person's skills or competency, but it is also dictated by the context in which the person has to create value and the information they hold about themselves. Firms could assist individuals in creating value within context. For example, some individuals find it very difficult to restrain themselves from eating too much. Creating solutions that help these individuals to exercise or count calories could empower them to work pro-actively on their weight loss routines.

Similarly, LaDiDa is an app that adds music and autotunes to your voice, making your voice sound better when you sing. The value proposition hinges on bringing musicality to large numbers of people who do not currently perform – potentially expanding the market and generating a wide range of revenues. This particular example is not currently free (the app download costs US$2.99) but the model could change to reflect the shifting sources of revenues. There are various software in use-contexts that could generate revenues even if your value proposition is free.

**Risk-based revenues.** Value creation is not the only mechanism through which firms can derive increased revenues. They can also do so through the manipulation of risk. Customers are willing to pay more if they perceive risks to be higher, or if they are deprived of the product or service with which to create value. Therefore, even if exchange is not in the same time and space as use, individuals may be willing to pay more when they think that there might be limited capacity. The creation and amplification of risk can be seen all around us. Limited editions of things, the scarcity of certain commodities, the unavailability of capacity in a football stadium or concert venue, all contribute towards heightening perceived risk which in turn allows the firm to charge more.

## MARKET INCENTIVE MECHANISMS

As I mentioned previously, revenues are derived from the whole market. Since total revenues are the focal point for viability, we need to understand how to create revenues from a heterogeneous market of value creators at the point of exchange. This means we could create worth at different price points for different people. This practice is commonly labelled as 'price discrimination'.

In the traditional economy, what was important was exchange. How we went about *using* offerings and objects were pretty much opaque to everyone. Unless firms did market research to understand how people used their offerings, not many understood value created in use and experience. Even so, market research tends to look at use in the way it influences the purchase or design of the offering. Most of all, economics and market research tend to look only at use to profile their market in terms of people who buy, rather than the *contexts* of use. There is a big difference between the two.

For example, you could say the use of the kettle is for 'tea-making' as a context or you can say the use of the kettle is for 'a person who likes to make tea'. This leads to different assumptions and opportunities for kettle-makers. In the former, the focus for value creation is on contexts. In the latter, the focus is to profile who might buy a kettle. Both are necessary, as the distinctiveness of a person and his or her behaviour are both part of the context. In the traditional economic world, only the distinctiveness of a person is important,

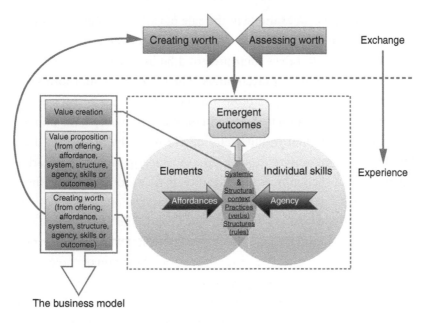

FIGURE 9.1: Business model, exchange and value creation

which is why we profile and segment markets based on segments of individuals. In a contextual value-creating digital world, we could be segmenting markets based on segments of contexts (see Figure 9.1).

Thus, by understanding contexts for value creation and the practices involved, firms can segment based on contextual archetypes. If we charge for use or experience, could we not charge differently for different contexts of experience rather than for different people? For example, if we create conditional access, there are some contexts of experience where we could give more access and some less regardless of the person. This is already happening with some publishers where individuals would need to pay more to access a newspaper online, even if they are already subscribers on another channel. If we decide to bend some rules for some contexts and not for others, we could create differential price points for the market to choose which contexts they prefer. How do we then think about separating different contexts so that we can derive revenues from different price points?

Let me give an example of the sale of garlic. In many supermarkets, garlic can be found in various forms; loose where the customer has the freedom to select their preferred bulbs, pre-selected bulbs in packets, peeled bulbs, or diced bulbs. The price of the four forms are usually different, with premiums on the latter three. If one were to randomly choose a hundred customers, the firm would have no idea which of the hundred would prefer one form to the other. Yet if all hundred customers were to walk into the supermarket to buy garlic, the market for each form would separate. Perhaps some may not know how to choose garlic and would prefer pre-packed ones, while others may not like the smell of garlic on their hands and choose the diced option. Others may have high time costs and do not want to waste their time on choosing garlic. Whatever the reason, the menu of choices has performed a major function of segmenting, separating and immediately targeting the market with discriminating prices between individuals. Since the individuals self-select the segment they belong to, there is no cannibalisation. That means we do not need to hide any of the price points from everyone – we merely let them choose. What was previously private information (which form of garlic you prefer) has been revealed to the firm, which is able to obtain a price premium from the segment that is *willing* to pay that extra through self-selection.

Consider another example, of a retailer in a ski resort with a local population. The retailer could sell bottled water at €1 to the local population but the retailer loses the opportunity to charge wealthy ski vacationers a premium at €2 which they are quite willing to pay. If the retailer prices high, vacationers will buy but locals will probably go down the mountain to stock up. Normally, the optimal solution is to trade off and decide which segment would generate higher revenues – selling to x local population at €1 or to y population of vacationers at €2. However, there is a win-win incentive mechanism. Charging €2 for a bottle of water at the shop and placing a coupon in the local newspaper for a €1 discount would enable the retailer to get the best of both worlds and separate the market quite effectively (Moorthy, 1984). Even if the vacationers know about the coupon, they won't be bothered because they are quite happy to pay €2 to begin with, and cutting coupons would just not be worth the effort (Ng, 2006).

This segmentation tactic through self-selection originated from the economics concept of a 'designed contract', a menu for compensating an individual who possesses more information than the individual who offers the contract. By choosing a contract from a menu, individuals with more information reveal the truth about their preferences (Moorthy, 1984). From the menu, individuals choose to buy different pairs, thus revealing what they truly value (Akerlof, 1970; Rothschild & Stiglitz, 1976).

The above examples look at separating groups for different price points at the point of exchange. However, as exchanges and experiential contexts start coming together, the ability to separate groups at different price points to generate higher *total* revenues comes from understanding the variety and heterogeneity of contexts, and then designing incentive mechanisms and choice menus to create worth. In the future, choices in buying and using would reveal many more differences between contextual archetypes, and firms could then segment based on individuals' needs to deeply personalise, due to the variety exhibited by practices, rules, individual skills, agencies and other elements in context. However, instead of segmenting to sell, firms can also recreate and redesign scalable offerings for deep personalisation. Since exchange is always held before the experience and worth is to be created at the point of exchange, the firm has to examine closely its offering for exchange and the time/space relationship between the exchange and the experience.

## VALUE AND WORTH: A DIVIDE

Recall that in Chapter 5, I mentioned that we don't often pay for outcomes, even though achieving the outcome is the reason we buy things. Industries have existed for a few hundred years believing in the alignment between value and worth because creating value can only come from firms creating worth. We got the outcomes we wanted from the products we bought, and the firms got the money they needed to make more of it. We were one happy economic family in a closed system. The firm had little visibility of what exactly you were doing with the things you bought, and since your use of them spurred little follow-on economic exchange, they weren't that interested anyway.

This happy state of usage ignorance started to change with digitisation and connectivity. We started to create more value with just a few products and services, e.g., broadband, laptop, installed software, mobile phone, 3G; something economists call *externalities*. As more people used them and we became more connected, these few offerings started to make our lives better. And this was without having to buy more because they became convenient channels to connect with other people and obtain more information as part of an external benefit, and often for free. Through the Internet, we are able to access many more services and information without paying for them.

The fundamental issue is that with digital connectivity, there are greater external benefits, i.e., we are now able to create much more value from single points of exchange of offerings, and yet the value we create (the external benefit) is less able to be translated to worth for firms. Of course, other firms benefit from the externality in the form of new offerings, but the firm that creates the original offering does not often benefit from continuing revenues, unless its business model allows for it. Where before, the value we create with a single desktop computer was expected and static (we can do word processing, calculate on spreadsheets and do presentations), worth and value were more aligned. Today, a desktop computer can do much more through connectivity and create more value (i.e., goodness) for us, but that does not become internalised into greater revenues for the firm.

After a while, other digital offerings came along that could help us connect with even more people. We started to receive services from other people, sometimes for free. Then a whole economy of new services came about that harvested the connectivity. These services were provided through the cloud and apps that, although requiring the use of devices to access them, didn't really pay the device seller for this use. The Google search engine is a case in point. To access Google requires connectivity (e.g., broadband) and a device (e.g., a laptop), but neither the customer nor Google paid directly for that service. For the customer, the costs are often 'sunk', which means broadband providers and laptop sellers have already been compensated. Creating value for individuals is becoming dependent on a whole value constellation of objects and services, and trying to commodify that value-creating system is a challenge for all the connected entities in the constellation.

As platforms emerge to capture the information exchange, interactions and even entertainment, firms struggle to think about how to derive revenue from markets and possible exchanges. It is towards markets, commodification and new economic models that, in the last chapter, I now turn.

## CHAPTER 9 REFLECTIONS

Never mind the quality – feel the width.

The comedic 'size matters' tag line lives on as firms look with despair at their cost-plus pricing models for products where market scale is limited. Commercial viability demands either cost reduction or a massively increased market, or both.

With digitisation, we can see this with music downloads and apps that appeal to millions of users at modular costs that would previously have been unimaginable. The issue is not how much the customer is willing to pay, but how much the firm is willing (or able) to scale to bring in revenues (directly or indirectly) from a vastly wider market.

Along with the old cost-plus ideas, we can also see the 1980s notion of competitive advantage being usurped by collaborative advantage – once again, in that arena of Arno Penzias's *Harmony* and interoperability.

The landscape of fabrication is changing – customisation choices, 3D printing, the wholesale mixing and matching of digital options . . . old hands might say 'you couldn't make it up'! Except, now you can – and firms must find new revenue models for creating worth from value creation.

It helps, of course, if you own (or create) the platform and eventually reap the rewards when (or if) your design becomes part of the connected culture. The long road to success taken by Amazon, Google, Facebook, Skype and others is a journey of continual reinvention and learning as they tread carefully around the fallen bodies of those who didn't adapt fast enough.

In the gaps unserved by established platforms are new revenue opportunities through gatekeeping and through shifts in the rules – hard changes in legislation and softer shifts in behaviours. Among the many gaps are weaknesses in skills – our individual agency – constraining value creation. It is hardly a surprise to see new markets in education, certification and accreditation.

In all these battles to create commercial viability it becomes clear that for individuals, creating value is increasingly dependent on the prevailing mix of multiple services and facilities – an entire 'value constellation' of objects and services.

This is not just the challenge of your firm. To create worth from that value-creating system is a challenge for *all* the connected entities in the constellation. Working together – this emergence of open collaboration – may well be beyond your experience or beyond your comfort zone.

But, if not with you, who?

# 10 Markets, digital labour and new economic models

> We are not prisoners of an inevitable future. Uncertainty makes us free.
>
> Peter Bernstein, Against the Gods

A market is any structure that allows entities to exchange any type of goods, services and information. This could happen in a playground, such as for trading cards or baseball cards, online such as on eBay, or in a formal place such as the London Stock Exchange. A market could therefore be participated in by institutions and individuals, and it could subscribe or conform to procedures, social relations and infrastructures so that all parties could engage in exchange. Markets become available when people need resources and when firms are given access to operate. In New York, if you queue up on a hot day to enter the Empire State Building, there is a market for drinking water and usually, within five minutes, a street vendor will appear to sell you a bottle. On the other hand, I may be on a plane with a need for some really good coffee but coffee providers usually have no access to planes, so while there is a need, no market is possible.

It is tempting to think of a market as a system where the value that society wishes to create with the offerings being acquired is equivalent to the money given to firms. That, unfortunately, is an oversimplification because it assumes that the market is efficient in its allocation, i.e., firms produce only offerings that are desirable in the society, and there is high demand and low prices, i.e., the market is free and perfectly competitive. Unfortunately, that is not usually the case. In any economic system, allocation of resources results in 'winners' and 'losers' and there is often 'friction'. Firms endeavour to 'game' the market as part of their role as profit-driven organisations, and this results in different market structures such as oligopolies or monopolistic markets. Welfare economists use 'allocative efficiency' as a benchmark to evaluate different market structures and public policies to understand which subgroups are being made better or worse off.

The structure of and boundaries between firms and markets are generally studied in Industrial Organisation (IO) Economics, building on the theory of the firm. The objective of IO studies is to improve the understanding of how firms and industries operate, to increase industries' contribution to economic welfare, and to improve government policy toward these industries. Some IO economists have been actively advising firms on how to improve their conduct and performance, under different market structures. The Internet has also led to a proliferation of IO research in two major areas. The first is the two- or multi-sided markets. The second is network effects. Each will be explained in turn.

## MULTI-SIDED MARKETS

When we go to the supermarket, it may seem like we have many choices but actually, these are only choices to buy and not choices to use. In the early days, if I had chickens and my neighbour had ducks, a market would be formed to exchange chickens for ducks. As others joined in, we could get everything we wanted from the market as long as we had something to trade. When it became clear that it was just inefficient to use what we had to trade because not everyone wanted my chickens and I had to trade with ducks just to get the vegetables, money came along (this is, of course, the simplified version). Money was efficient of course, even though it does have its moral limits (Sandel, 2000). What we have forgotten though, is that we always *brought* our offerings to a market. In the days of barter, we had to bring our offerings to the market (usually down river, to the delta where other buyers are around), commodify them for worth, and then bring something back into context to realise the value.

In more recent times, on the demand side, this meant we had to also go out to the shops or go online to a website with our money, seek out what we want, buy it and bring it back to the context of use. Economists call this 'search costs'. What has not been said, though, is that since I buy it out of context, I have to strip off all my contextual needs. Instead of thinking about having my hair clean which includes the elements of water, shower, towel, I am forced into a reductionistic thought of the institutionalised solution of just shampoo because that's what I go out to the market to buy. If we see how our mobile phone that began as a simple communication device has changed in terms of its usage, we can see why our needs in context could be served better if we had objects that understood our system of value creation rather than just being objects.

Every firm tries to do that of course. We see many types of shampoo in the market, all to ensure that as much variety of use in context as possible is catered for. This is called a single-sided market, where the firm, whether a shampoo company or a paint manufacturer, serves a population of customers. Even if the market consists of multiple segments, they do not interact with one another and would only buy from the firm. This is because the firm believes it can cater to as many types of variety as the customer would like. However, when serving customers becomes too prohibitive in terms of costs due to hyper-variety, market forces could cause the creation of two-sided or multi-sided markets from single-sided markets.

Two-sided markets are places where both buyers and sellers gather because of each other, rather than to trade with the firm. This creates enough variety (through a market) to serve customers' needs. A platform emerges, creating favourable conditions for exchanges to happen which could be controlled by the same firm or which could have disrupted the original offering. Markets are efficient in this way. For example, mobile phone users were part of a single-sided market served by the likes of Nokia. Early mobile phones had only text messaging, calendar, alarm and perhaps a camera. As their use became more ubiquitous and complex, customers demanded more functionality and greater personalisation. The demand for high variety in use and experiential contexts grew, and it became increasingly difficult for Nokia to provide more services on its mobile phones.

Apple entered the market, and instead of controlling the apps and creating a different iPhone for everyone, Apple's solution was to draw its market boundary around a scalable platform and let developers provide apps for customers, creating a two-sided market for app providers and customers, even while tightly regulating both sides' use of the platform. And by being a provider itself, Apple's platform became multi-sided. This meant the demand for the platform sky-rocketed as more customer varieties were able to be served. Interestingly, Apple did not do this deliberately at the beginning. It allowed software developers onto the phone platform because it felt that its core competency was in hardware manufacturing, and Apple's mental model was that of the personal computer – it made the kit and let others put on the software. Today, there are more than 700,000 apps available for Apple's iOS platform as well as for the Android platform.[1] Market demand soared because individual varieties were able to be served. Mobile phone-makers that did not respond quickly enough to the hyper-variety demands of the market got left behind.

A traditional fresh produce market is *two-sided* because more sellers will come if there are more buyers, and conversely, more customers will do so if there are more sellers. *Multi-sided* markets mean that service is rendered both from the platform and from the participants, e.g., the people who own the market provide some sort of platform service to all the buyers and sellers, such as home delivery of purchases. Two-sided and multi-sided markets face the challenge of creating a critical mass so that all sides would come together. Revenue models where one side will get the service for free so that the other side will also come have become the norm under such markets, not unlike allowing ladies into clubs for free so that men will come along too.

---

[1] news.cnet.com/8301-1035_3-57542502-94/google-ties-apple-with-700000-android-apps/. Accessed 1 July 2013

Multi-sided markets face three problems:

- the chicken-and-egg dilemma of how long and how much to subsidise one side before the other side hits critical mass;
- when both sides hit critical mass, determining what keeps both sides interested to stay; and
- what is commodifiable for the platform to continue its service and viability. Multi-sided markets become useful when hyper-variety of contexts become untenable.

Traditional single-sided industries such as music licensees that made their money through scarcity and ownership of the license have not taken this well. Music cannot be shared, some say, without giving revenues back to the owners. Most music licensees would have preferred to keep the market one-sided but the demand for variety in music-sharing and experience has become too high to be served by a single-sided market. Firms such as Spotify, Deezer and Shazam have become multi-sided market platforms for sharing, buying and listening music, and music licensees will have to cope with a distributed worth of music through such platforms when more customers sign up to these firms.

Music tells the story of markets. Before we buy anything, we will usually search (Pissarides, 1985). The economic idea of search is based on the fact that there is always a 'carrier' of search, and it is important that this search occurs in a place that is free so that offerings can compete to be the best to serve us. For economists, the marketplace is a carrier of search. It is the 'substrate' characterised by freedom of physical movement – it is not a metaphor for some other concept. Economists think of economic agents as going to an actual market, and physically searching market stalls before deciding what to buy (or sell) and how much to buy (or sell). Importantly (for economists), such carriers of search, i.e., the substrates, do not impede competition, which is in turn crucial for a proper allocation of resources (Levin, 2013).[2]

With better technological possibilities to serve contexts, consumers will demand to be served closer and closer to lived lives, and new firms will find ways to create offerings to serve those needs. New markets and new substrates will begin to flourish, not merely on mobile phones, but also at homes, buildings, trains, buses and places where we live contextual lives. Think about the old days when vendors got onto trains at a station and stayed onboard to sell you water, food, etc., leaping off onto the platform just before the train left. In the future, your table on the train could be used as an interface to connect you to the train and its information, and serve all the needs you might have while on the train. This is inevitable because our search costs are lowest, and our willingness to pay the highest (barring risks and other transaction costs), when firms can come to us instead of us going to them.

However, as we have learnt from the music industry, the train offering in itself will change. Digital backwash onto the train is inevitable as well because once an offering decides to serve us in context, it has to deal with *how* it *should change* to serve us in context so that the train sits within a value-creating system with connections to other things. Where an offering cannot deal with the variety that comes from serving us in context, other firms may be able to do so with their offerings, and achieve competitive advantage. All objects

---

[2] My thanks to Kimberley Scharf for helping me explain this so succinctly

that could be connected will need to sit on platforms for multi-sided markets to enable both exchange and experiential use in the future.

## NETWORK EFFECTS

Every voluntary market exchange is always mutually beneficial to both sides of the trade. This is because there wouldn't be an exchange otherwise. However, exchanges can cause additional effects. As mentioned previously, such effects are called *externalities*. In economics, an externality is a cost or benefit that is not a consequence of the exchange mechanism, and is incurred by an entity that was not involved in the exchange that caused the cost or benefit. The cost of an externality is an external cost, while the benefit of an externality is an external benefit. For example, external costs could be the depletion of fish stocks while a firm is harvesting fish. External costs are the negative environmental impacts on such depletion. On the other hand, external benefits could be the control of an infectious disease by a public body thereby preventing others from getting ill. Welfare economics has shown that the existence of externalities results in outcomes that are not always socially optimal. Those who suffer from external costs cannot help it, while those who enjoy external benefits get them for free. While this might be appealing to some of us, not being able to internalise external benefits could lead to inefficient allocation because fewer jobs are created.

*Network* externalities (Shapiro & Varian, 1999) occur where there is a change (usually an increase) in the benefit that an individual derives from an offering, when the number of other individuals using the same offering changes. In other words, the value you gain from using or experiencing something is dependent on how many others are doing so as well. Companies such as Facebook are dependent on network externalities – as indeed were early telephone companies before the standards for interconnection enabled market expansion. Network externalities can be both positive and negative. Negative network externalities could occur, e.g., when too many people are using an exclusive brand which may cheapen its image.

When externalities are internalised, e.g., brought back into market exchanges, they are no longer externalities but merely effects. Internalisation of externalities is important so that the economy benefits as a whole.

Network effects can be categorised as direct or indirect (Katz & Shapiro, 1994). Direct network effects occur when you get the benefit of a product directly because others are using it as well. Telephones fall into that category. Indirect effects occur when we get the benefit of an offering not from the usage of the same offering by others, but because of the other peripheral offerings that are developed in support of the consumption of others. For example, you may not get the benefit of more people watching satellite TV, but if so many are watching such that the service provider starts to add new and free channels, you would benefit. These new and free channels would actually entice more people to sign up for satellite TV, thereby internalising the network effect.

Society has benefited greatly from network effects of digital offerings, directly and indirectly. Among many other benefits, consumer welfare is increased because of greater choice and reduced information costs. Digital connectivity has made us share and collaborate more. A rather obscure Korean song, *Gangnam Style*, went viral on YouTube in 2012 with 480 million views across the world within four months, and propelled singer Psy to fame; he appeared in talk shows from Australia to the US. When US Presidential candidate Mitt Romney made a gaffe during a presidential debate in 2012, the Internet went crazy with Twitter and Facebook accounts created within minutes.

Digital connectivity is no longer just a productivity tool. It has become a lifestyle, amusement, entertainment and quality-of-life necessity. Economists believe that a positive externality that increases our welfare at no cost to us improves collective societal welfare, but if firms have no way of internalising these effects (i.e., monetising the effects through the creation of worth and new revenues), the result could be that the economy is less efficient. If market pricing mechanisms don't work, we might find that only a few of us are better off, but with firms not benefiting from internalising these effects, less production occurs and jobs are not created. This is becoming the case with the rise of the digital economy. However, I argue that while we see the reduction of jobs, we will also see the rise of start-ups and entrepreneurs.

## SPIRALLING DIGITAL DEMAND

Figure 10.1 shows the spiralling effect of exchanges in the digital economy.

First, a digital offering's ability to serve contexts and dynamic demands results in value creation in context that includes socialisation and connectivity. Our ability to create value-in-context and connect with others results in *latent needs* emerging in context. RunKeeper is an app that uses GPS to track our fitness runs and keep a record of them online. We can share the results and in doing so, alert others to the app. Seeing the success of RunKeeper, firms may develop other digital offerings that can connect to it, and these may be

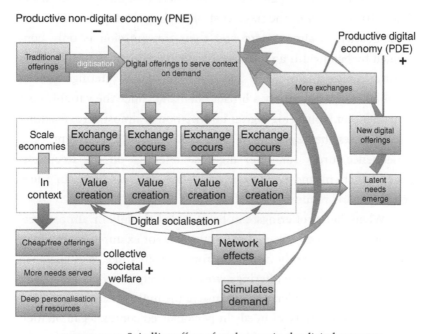

FIGURE 10.1: Spiralling effect of exchanges in the digital economy

purchased by the existing RunKeeper market as well as attracting new ones.

As a subscriber to Spotify, for example, being able to play my music offline means I can listen to it while driving to work. While this makes me happy, it has created a latent need for music recommendations as I would like to change my driving tracks weekly. As more latent needs are met, others will emerge and we demand newer ways to serve us, resulting in even more digitised offerings.

Second, socialisation in the digital space creates network effects, making existing individuals even better off after purchase. These *network effects* are internalised (monetised) back into the economic system as consumers buy more digital offerings. We now hear of firms using crowd-funding, crowd-sourcing and open innovation as ways of internalising these network effects.

Third, firms are able to cater to a surge in demand because of the *scalability* of digitised offerings. Digits have almost infinite economies of scale. They cannot be 'used up' (Negroponte, 1995). While not everything can be digitised, the production of digital offerings is almost 100 per cent of the fixed cost of sending the first bit. The cost of duplication is almost zero and their transmission is only constrained by bandwidth and access. By digitising part, if not all, of an offering, economies of scale and scope in digital offerings can be exploited in order to satisfy a broader demand. Since the variable cost component for replicating digital information is almost zero, reaching scale becomes the key for increasing the return on investment. As a consequence, firms can offer digitised offerings on the freemium model which means we often get it for free, resulting in more 'purchases' and reinforcing the freemium model.

When digital offerings can be provided cheaply or almost free, more of society can be served at a low cost. For example, so much of what we know is freely available from websites like Wikipedia. In addition, many of these offerings work on a ubiquitous platform such as a smartphone or tablet, and because of the multi-sided nature of the market, greater variety of needs in personalised contexts can be met. The ability for firms to serve and personalise for our variety of needs allows us to demand for entertainment, assistance and knowledge anywhere and everywhere. Indeed, increasing channels to interact seem to trigger what Clay Shirky (2010) calls 'cognitive surplus', where our free time is now being used more creatively. We have moved from being passive consumers to becoming empowered and actively sharing content with others. This in turn creates more productive gains for ourselves. This *external benefit* then stimulates further demand for more digital offerings.

With network effects, scale economies from digitisation, external benefits from cheap offerings and the personalisation and emergence of more latent needs, we are seeing much greater social benefits in the digital economy, and the collective societal welfare improves. It is no wonder that digitisation and connectivity have been acknowledged the world over to provide significant benefits to society, and these benefits are evidential justification for countries to invest heavily in fibre optics and connected technologies.

However, as latent needs surface to demand more service in context, more traditional offerings become disrupted and absorbed into the digital economy. We now do not need to buy a lot of things. Our mobile phone now provides us with a dictionary, compass, torchlight, and diary; many things which were not digital before but have now become so. This thing that we call a phone has become a personal remote control for our individual choices of engagement in the digital economy.

Digital disruptions to traditional non-digital objects are starting to 'demonetise' the traditional non-digital economy while increasing exchanges in the digital economy. Many apps are provided on a freemium model. Even objects that we think may not be easily duplicated are now being reinvented as digital alternatives. For example, Cardiio is an iPhone app that measures your heart rate. The iPhone does not have a sensor technology to measure your pulse but it seems that every time our hearts beat, more blood is pumped into our faces thus increasing the blood volume, leading to more light being absorbed. Cardiio's software can detect changes in reflected light from our faces and if we look into the iPhone front-facing camera, the app can calculate our heartbeat.

Disrupting the traditional economy has created a reallocation of a different kind. The firms that benefit from the disruptions are the start-ups and entrepreneurs, and not the traditional firms. This creates a temporary imbalance in the sense that the number of jobs in the economy may be reduced, but the number of start-ups and entrepreneurs increases while collective societal welfare is improved.

Not all disruptions result in the loss of market share in the material economy. Traditional firms that learn to digitise their offerings to be able to serve contexts pre-emptively and strategically may be able to innovate their way towards the future and internalise some of the benefits. This is especially true on the mobile platform. In the past, the Internet economy played itself out on desktops and laptops. Except for Facebook and social networks, the Internet was largely dominated by informational and sales channels because while the Internet could be *part* of our lives, its lack of mobility did not *intervene* in our lives – i.e., it wasn't present everywhere.

Moving into the mobile realm changed that. Mobile platforms meant the Internet had access to contexts of lived lives and could potentially intervene in our lives to offer us better service wherever and whenever we required. That is why a mobile phone has a torchlight app while computers never had it. If you are faced with a sudden blackout, chances are your phone is with you and it could intervene to offer a resource. Manufacturers of objects could learn how their offerings can be modified to create better and more connected experiences in customer lives, enabling them to change their business models to create revenues more aligned with customer's outcomes. Already, some industries are considering signing up to platforms so that they can connect with other objects and services in order to internalise greater value creation, to create worth for their own offerings.

Whoever controlled the platform inevitably became the gatekeeper and benefited from the emergence of latent needs in contexts by being able to offer new services. The smartphone as a technological platform is increasingly a dominant market platform, and it dictates the market structure in which other vendors participate even while the platforms battle among themselves. The intense competition between Apple and Samsung in the smartphone category is not merely for control of smartphone market share, but essentially for domination of the space to serve us in context. As I have mentioned before, this space will be dominated by the need for a widget (e.g., smartphone), community, content and connectivity. Industries that play in these four strategic areas will be battling it out in the future.

From a societal welfare perspective, the optimal market solution is not to hinder gatekeepers but to create more of them. Indeed, other platforms are emerging. There is talk of smart homes, smart cities and smart buildings, and these are potential platforms to serve buyers and their needs. However, there is a lack of understanding of how a technological platform could be configured as a market platform. The aspiration is that a home or a building could be like a smartphone, with an information hub of connected things and sensors, and there will be digital offerings sitting on the platform to serve us at home and within the building. For example, if the kettle and your smart home are connected, you could boil water for tea before you get home. As home and building become smart market platforms, our concept of apps would evolve to become 'thing-apps' (thapps?) where instead of apps that serve us in context, we have connected things that could do more with us, and for us.

However, most people who talk about such smart platforms do not consider the market structure of the platform. Digitisation of economic activity enables new business models to emerge, along with new forms of cooperation and new types of coordination mechanisms within the economic incentive system. The emerging networked economy is significantly changing market structures and firm behaviours. This brings about changes in various levels of IO. Current economic literature is inadequate to understand completely the nature of the dynamics of such an economy. The conventional neo-classical theory uses a 'representative firm', and some 'representative good or service' for exchange, which is an oversimplification of a connected exchange economy. The behaviour of the firm in such analyses is often not affected by direct interdependencies with other entities. There is very little explanation given to explain the dynamics and collaborative advantages that are created by increasing interconnectivity between firms through digital networks. Conventional economics research attempting to reduce a whole system to what can be explained has compelled many to search for answers to explain the implications of direct and indirect interdependencies in a digitally connected economy.

It is certain that the world will see a redistribution of wealth, between those which are engaged in a digital economy, and those who are not. Feminist political economist of labour Ursula Huws discussed how the invention of motor cars displaced workers from coach-building but created jobs in the manufacturing of cars (Huws et al., 1999). With mass production, jobs were lost in car-making, resulting in more jobs created in services such as design, research and development, marketing, finance, insurance and legal services. These roles changed with greater information technology, displacing clerks, managers and accountants but creating new jobs in information technology, computer-assisted design, call centres and financial management. We are now at the next wave of job destruction and job (entrepreneurial?) replacement but this time, because of digital scalability and commodification as I will explain shortly, this change might be the most disruptive of all.

## COMMODIFICATION

By far the most controversial aspect of the digital economy is its potential for commodification. *Commodification* (a term which dates back to 1975, believed to have originated from Marxist political theory) is used to describe the process by which something with no economic worth is assigned some worth. This is different from *commoditisation* which is when an offering moves towards undifferentiated competition. The Italian economist Piero Sraffa once said that firms are involved in 'the production of commodities by means of commodities' (Sraffa, 1960), which means that firms make offerings based on what is offered to firms. This line of thinking of course has led to the commodification of many aspects of life that some consider excessive. Our dreams, our fears, our stem cells have been commodified to become offerings of status, security and hope. Back in 1994 before the proliferation of the Internet, Dallas Smythe considered TV audiences as commodities. By watching advertisements, the audiences 'work' for the media by letting themselves be marketed to and by doing so, media firms mass produce audiences and 'sell' them to advertisers (Smythe, 1981). Audiences therefore 'labour' for distribution and consumption of things produced. The moral limits of commodification have also been widely discussed (Sandel, 2000).

The digital economy has seen a proliferation of commodification practices since many of our value-creating activities have become digitally visible. We click on ads suggested by Google, write information on Wikipedia, update our status on Facebook, tweet about our lives and our opinions, and upload videos on YouTube. With our lives becoming more digitally visible, we produce more data about ourselves even as we consume more digital offerings. We become 'prosumers', a term coined by Alvin Toffler (1984) to describe a consumer who produces as well as consumes. This thinking has been extended to the digital realm where the digital self becomes 'digital labour' through digital value-creating practices (Manzerolle, 2010). The technical, functional and social capabilities of mobile media mean that there are more varied forms of commodifying our digital labour practices (Hearn, 2008). We contribute 'creative', 'intellectual' and 'emotional' labour through the way we interact (Cohen, 2008; Fuchs, 2009).These digital labour practices are made ever more possible through smartphones. Musicovery is an app that categorises your music collection on your smartphone and plays music to you according to your mood, in degrees of 'dark', 'positive', 'energetic' or 'calm' modes. While doing so, your mood becomes part of digital labour. Indeed, our digital labour spawns even more digital labour through the need to maintain our digital identities and social networks. Firms learn about their customers through the collection of their personal data, and repackage the data to sell on to other firms. There are many out there who have been campaigning to protect the rights of the increasingly perilous, alienated, exploited digital 'labourer', arguing that commodification of digital labour dehumanises us.

I make a distinction between creating worth and commodification. Commodification is the translation of something, usually an activity, effort or asset into money. Commodification of labour is therefore translating work, whether skilled on unskilled, into money. From that commodification, the firm creates worth into the market, usually by leveraging on capital and technology to produce an offering. Creating worth is the creation of an offering that can receive revenues.

Commodification of labour or digital labour does not automatically assume that worth is created. Worth creation is part of the business model and the firm's capability to compete in markets. Worth however includes a portion of the commodification of labour and what economists would call surplus value, which is the firm's ability (through labour) to create an offering such that markets will pay more than the cost of producing it (Table 10.1).

There are two ideological positions you can take at this point. From a labour economics point of view, surplus value is only created because of labour and should therefore return to labour, and from a

capitalist point of view, surplus value is the firm's ability to combine technology, capital and labour to produce and create worth from offerings, so surplus value should belong to the firm's shareholders. There is no wrong or right – merely your ideological standpoint. In reality, the outcome is

Table 10.1 *Digital labour: what has been commodified*

| What has been commodified | Commodified activity | Potential worth created |
|---|---|---|
| Your interest (through fingers, eyeballs and ears) | Clicks on advertisements, listening to ads, vote on TV shows | Segmentation and targeting algorithms for advertisers |
| Your credibility (through endorsement) | 'Likes', recommendations, endorsements, reviews | Segmentation and targeting algorithms for advertisers, promotion of offering |
| Your time (through waiting) | Waiting | Increase efficiency and revenues from prioritisation |
| Your personal information (through data) | Giving up information on buying behaviour, use behaviours, daily life, status updates, polls | Segmentation and targeting algorithms for advertisers, promoting offerings |
| Your knowledge (through content generated) | Creating YouTube videos, writing blogs, writing tweets | Promoting offerings, improvement to design of offering, feedback |
| Your mood | Sharing music | Segmentation and targeting algorithms for advertisers |
| Your skill | Creating virtual skill levels in online games | Selling new virtual assets |

usually what the economists would call a 'bargaining solution', as it is manifested in much of modern economic systems today.

NEW ECONOMIC MODELS FOR PERSONAL DATA

As the digital age progresses further, more of ourselves can now be potentially commodified. I say potentially, because it depends on the firm's ability to do so. For practices that are measurably visible and direct such as mouse clicks and button presses, its commodification potential is obvious. Companies like Google or Facebook have sophisticated algorithms to calculate how much a recommendation, a share or a like, could translate to creating worth for advertisers. However, since digital connectivity also allows us to interact, we are now digitally more visible – we vote, pay and applaud, and the commodification of such practices is much more of a challenge. With greater digitisation into the contexts of homes and buildings, the digital self in the future could be seen more transparently through how we create value within digital contexts, i.e., the visibility of elements (nouns), system (verbs), structures (rules), agency, affordance and outcomes in contexts.

We already generate much personal data through our financial transactions, tax records, health behaviours and online interactions. There is growing concern over our ability to control what information we reveal about ourselves over the Internet, and who can access that information. The US Federal Trade Commission has provided a set of guidelines on widely accepted concepts concerning fair information practices in electronic exchanges called the Fair Information Practice Principles. The problem is that treating data according to what is 'good practice' doesn't allay individuals' reservations about its collection and use. It breeds a culture of mistrust, especially when so much of what we need to do digitally results in signing 'informed consent' about what firms could do with our data, documents that we cannot humanly process in terms of their implications. In addition, injustice may arise because individuals could buy and use digital offerings under conditions of inequality or necessity which suggest that such practices are coercive, prompted by the necessities of the situation.

How should we understand our personal data in terms of privacy, vulnerability and security for ourselves on one hand, while on the other hand we would like firms to create new offerings to serve us in context? How should we think of personal data protection while at the same time allowing this data to enable the creation of new markets?

These are the conditions we often face today with online personal data privacy:

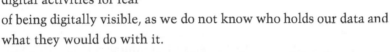

- We withhold our consent for personal data to be used because we get nothing in return.
- We do not wish to participate in online digital activities for fear of being digitally visible, as we do not know who holds our data and what they would do with it.
- The firm refuses to compensate for use of personal data because it does not know yet what worth (new offerings) could be created.
- The firm owns our data and could do with it what they wish, as long as they anonymise it. But they cannot share it with another party unless it is anonymised, so there is limited understanding of the data.

One way of thinking about personal data is to start from the position that it is our digital labour. Thus, allowing it to be owned by someone else such as a firm is allowing for its exploitation, regardless of how the firm anonymises it. This does not mean that firms cannot be allowed access; merely that the information could be made freely accessible by the individuals who generate the data to begin with, since the data is coproduced with the firm. The reason this principle should exist is that personal data could then be seen as our labour for commodification, just as we see our real work in life as such. This creates a market for digital labour, of which firms could 'buy' and for which they could compensate individuals.

Taken to the extreme, digital labour (i.e., visible practices online) would then become an asset to individuals. By doing so, individuals may not be so restrained in our digital practices, since it is a reduction of our assets, but may be more discerning about whom we share them with. Thereby, we may share only when we are able to benefit from doing so. Currently, our compensation for personal data is often what is commonly known as a 'free lunch'. So we may get back coupons, discounts and freebies from the commodification of our digital practices. By liberating personal data into a format stored and accessible to firms, a market for 'prosumerism' exchanges could be created where individual choices can be respected while markets are created with new business models for compensation and experience.

This could be a viable solution because the current personal data held by several institutions is often not shareable under privacy rules. Thus different firms hold data that is partial and vertically siloed, providing incomplete visibility. This results in digital labour becoming less valuable to firms, and commodification becomes a challenge since firms do not yet know how to create worth from digital labour. Access to more complete visibility of the customer with suitable compensation for digital labour could create better offerings for individuals, allow choice and stimulate market creation under conditions of fairness and consent.

Personal data protection may therefore be seen to be not just a privacy or legal issue, but also about market exchanges of property rights and the external effects that could be obtained from the creation of such a market. Our consent is not merely an ethical dilemma. It is a right not to 'work' and a right therefore not to be digitally visible, but if we decide to be visible we could be rewarded for that just as labour is compensated through work. When a market of personal data generation and use is created, individuals may be more willing to do digital work as a result, or at least, allow for our data to be visible and accessible. By doing so, we are accumulating a potential resource for a commodification opportunity, with the firm playing the role of selling us a service and creating worth from that commodification.

Without such a market, individuals may withhold consent and firms, being unable to create worth from partial personal data, will not pay for it. With no incentive for participation, what economists would term as 'market failure' will occur.

Such thinking aligns with Coasean economics. Nobel laureate Ronald Coase (1960) suggested that it didn't matter who initially owned the property rights; in our case, digital labour. If there were no transaction costs, bargaining (i.e., the market) will lead to an efficient outcome. The condition of 'no transaction cost' is a challenge in the current state of the economy. Many firms currently own personal data, as current policies dictate ownership as belonging to the collector rather than the generator. Since the data belongs to the firm, and under privacy rules is unable to be shared in its raw identifiable form, the transaction costs of creating new offerings in return for the individual are high, because no other data of the same customer can be shared. For example, if we want to know the relationship between our finance data and health data (both of which are digitally available but sitting with different institutions), there isn't a market for an offering to consolidate these datasets as they are owned by the firms that collected them. This means that personal data continues to be stove-piped according to the 'verticals', e.g., media (TV), household products (shampoo and razors), food and consumables, etc.

This has led to many initiatives around 'big data', which anonymises data and aggregates it for sharing only at a level which preserves anonymity. However, the aggregation and anonymising of data diminishes its worth since it has been detached from our identity and from the point where the data was generated. This identity data could provide visibility of the 'horizontals', i.e., our usage of products in conjunction with other products. Without the horizontals, the industry verticals view only a part of the system of their product's value-creating activities, reinforcing the vertical stove pipes. The economics of systems suggest that partial systems have no worth to firms (Katz & Shapiro, 1994). With high transaction costs of sharing due to privacy concerns at the identity level and no horizontal personal data to complement this, new economic and business models and new offerings for a digitally connected economy are impeded from emerging to serve individuals.

While firms today talk about 'big data', data will grow even bigger with greater connectivity and the IoT. Creating accessibility of data to the generator so that a market can be formed to incentivise us to give it freely (and produce more) means we will get new services and more trade (and wealth) results, even while we recognise the rights of individuals. We will all benefit from better traffic information if we allow our individual travel data to be collected, aggregated and served back to help us with our travel plans, but we are less willing to share our personal diets. Yet, if there is a service to synthesise our personal diet with our grocery purchases, and help us make better decisions on what we should eat, we could be willing to buy it.

In a sense, anonymity of big data and its aggregation jeopardises the ability of firms to make sense of it, and severely diminishes its worth. Whatever data is generated often needs to be allowed to be transformed, synthesised and socially connected to socially identifiable activities at various stages by different market-based applications that could integrate both the verticals and the horizontals. Data needs to be disintermediated, i.e., teased apart to reveal how it is generated by individuals and objects, so that a market for a service is created at every stage of the intermediation and aggregation. By doing so, the transformation of the data becomes a role for markets. Businesses and services can be created to serve these markets and firms can retain their rights as data generators – as contributors of digital labour.

It is not surprising that both government and industry for the 'IoT' have for some time felt this need for data disintermediation. Only that they gave the symptom a different name: interoperability. There is a feeling among industry players that it is important to be interoperable because more applications, businesses and wealth are created from interoperability. There is therefore talk about 'standards' and 'regulation' to create interoperability.

In truth, interoperability is already here. With IPv6, the Internet is already the platform for interoperability between things.

But there is a great danger here. The notion of interoperability between devices and systems could demand a pre-judgement of what data may be required at whatever level of intermediation. Ultimately, it is for a customer to decide what solutions or services might require which sort of data and at which level. The horizontals are multi-tiered and could create businesses at each tier. Markets are created from interfaces between inconsistencies through a service provision. Things by themselves do not become consistent. Through our actions, we make things consistent to enable a good quality of life. New businesses and ideas also create consistency, if the substrate is free for competition to occur. What is crucial for the future is a freer market for disintermediated personal data/digital labour to be transformed by offerings to allow more of this to happen. If two things that are meant to be connected are useful to be connected, the market will resolve this through a service (yes, there is an app for that). It is not for regulators or standards agencies to intervene where an exchange could possibly exist. It is however, important that they create a market for firms to access so that exchanges can occur.

The current economic standing on privacy and markets for data is already providing an indication of the competitiveness of nations in the future. Nations with liberal privacy rules who wish to take advantage of the digitally connected future and the potential of IoT will create substrates that ride roughshod over personal data and privacy issues (no names to be mentioned), and firms will flourish on these platforms that seem to be 'free to play'. And we all know that there are more than enough people in the world who do not understand enough about violation of their privacy to support such platforms. There is no doubt in my mind that nations which have the most regulated privacy rules and very little understanding of markets and their role in commodification of personal data, will lose out, all in the name of protecting their citizens. These nations will lose out to new businesses and jobs, and their citizens will not benefit from better products and services. But it's alright, they say, because privacy is preserved in the only way that they know how. The irony is that in the end, the globalised market will still compromise personal data, as the services rendered from other nations will capture market share of the individuals of such regulated nations. The efficiency of markets dictates that the only way to beat the market is to be more efficient.

When the economy is based on an exchange of ownership, we create unlimited value (or not) from what we buy, since we own it and can use it without limitations. Traditional exchange economy for goods provided little visibility of value creation, especially for things. The economic system only measures worth and not the value created. As firms wish to appropriate more revenues from value creation and change their business models particularly in the digital economy, they may give up the ownership model or even models of revenue along the entire 'vertical' channel. Instead, they may look to business models that derive revenues from use or experience which are business models from the 'horizontals' *and* 'verticals', i.e., systemic business models. These systemic business models are created from the lateral dependencies of objects sitting within contexts. By creating worth from systemic business models, the firm opens itself up to other ways of creating value. Understanding personal data and how digital activities create value-in-context becomes a stimulus for new business models and new innovative offerings. When the lateral dependencies become more visible, firms can start dipping into different vertical industries for their own revenues.

This is the case for Google. Google recommodifies data from one value-creating context to create worth in a different value-creating context. Google is able to capture data on the way we search, but instead of asking us for compensation for the use of the search engine, our data is worth more when it is aggregated and sold to advertisers, while preserving our anonymity. Compensation is provided to us through more targeted search outcomes and ads. Under this model, our data could be worth more to other individuals or firms than to us. Such data may be useless to us personally, but in aggregate, they become more useful to others, especially when they could create worth in a different value-creating context. By allowing access to data with suitable compensation, there could be further models that create different offerings with due compensation for digital labour. Google's credit card for small businesses to help them with liquidity issues (as discussed in Chapter 8) epitomises how new business models are created from the system.

One other economic model that is emerging is the exchange of activities without traversing the economic system. Since a digitally connected system could create more value than firms are able to create worth, we can consider exchange of activities without the loss that comes when such activities are translated to money. Current market transactions provide visibility for resources that can be commodified. Life consists of interactions and exchanges that are often not commodified. We create meaning and interest in our lives not merely from the objects we purchase and use, but through interactions and exchanges that do not traverse the market. Rather than think about markets as existing out of context, which is only when resources can be commodified, we could think about exchanges that do not arrive at the commodified market. This means that we must consider value creation not merely for offerings that we acquire from the market, but for other resources as well. We must also consider decommodification of offerings because alternative channels may be more effective or efficient in helping us live our lives better.

The current economics of markets is therefore the economics of resources or interactions that can be commodified into money and financial exchanges. Under that layer of financial exchanges lie the dynamics of day-to-day mundane interactions surrounding the use of those offerings. To understand what makes the economic layer therefore, it is necessary to see what happens underneath, i.e., we need to see more of how we create goodness from these offerings – that unlit, less visible world – for within that world is where new exchanges and new market models may lie.

The current economics of markets assumes that commodification and exchange are the only means through which lives can be improved. In many instances, this is starting to change. Social networks such as Facebook are starting to epitomise the phenomenon where lives of people are made better through interactions and exchanges without traversing the economic layer. More digital offerings are creating value in people's lives without an understanding of how they can be 'monetised'– e.g., the legions of sites offering car-sharing or couch-surfing. This is the commodification challenge when contexts are being served, often through digital means, but without a better understanding of how and where economic exchanges could occur since many of such digital services come without any form of ownership. In a sense, this is already happening within the digital economic system. Since parties can connect and exchange resources, barter and sharing activities through social networks are on the rise.

As more information such as train schedules, music and TV programmes become digitised, there are other ways our lives can now be made better without owning things that are exchanged with money. The horizontal contexts could be interacting with one another without traversing through the vertical firms and industry. This means that with digitisation, money as an efficient transacting medium becomes less efficient, especially when commodification of resources touches on morality. You may not accept money in return for walking your neighbour's dog, for example, because it is an act of neighbourliness, rather than the commodification of your time and skill. You might, however, accept a return gesture of him mowing your lawn. Such bartering was seen to be inefficient in the past because of information asymmetry and search costs – you did not know what skills could be available to barter your skills against. However, with increasing connectivity and platforms to create communities (e.g., Facebook), asymmetry and search costs cease to be a problem. More of such sharing of activities and competencies create other external benefits such as community building and engagement. Whether these become internalised to turn into new offerings remain to be seen.

In the past, the proposition to create value came from the commodification of labour, with capital and technology. This remains the case for many industries; you cannot have food or beverage without its manufacturing and production. However, in the past, firms expected compensation for the proposition in terms of money. With digitisation, there are now several routes to compensate the firm. Instead of compensating the firm monetarily, we could opt to be more visible digitally, in the way we create value with their offerings. We could show the firm the way we experience the propositions, the knowledge we have, the skills we employ and the actions we take, and in so doing, the firm could choose to commodify these skills, hopefully with our consent.

This is the case with loyalty programmes offered by retailers like Tesco or Walmart, who collect data about our purchases so that they can understand us better and compensate us with discount coupons. The future of the digital economy may be a more extreme form of this. The legal framework and the digitally visible skills and actions could become a higher form of compensation compared to your money. As I discussed earlier, we already give Google compensation through our search data and when we click on ads, and they aggregate and commodify that to generate more revenues than we can possibly provide them even if we wanted to pay for searching. This spiralling commodification economy could generate more wealth than the direct exchange economy. Of course, this is an extreme view. However, if we hypothetically adopt this view, it has three major implications:

- First, our future 'wealth' may not be just our money. It may include our digital skills, actions and competencies but only if they are able to be visible and commodifiable, and only if they are used subject to your consent and with due compensation.
- Second, the new wealth now sits within those who are most digitally connected and who make available their competencies for commodification as well as for sharing with others. They should get the most compensation when firms create worth through new offerings and when competencies can be traded. The latent wealth therefore belongs to the world's most connected and digitally visible people, who are able to trade their visibility for their own

goals and outcomes – a powerful argument for greater societal efforts to increase levels of digital participation. From the perspective of national wealth, the future rich will be the most digitally connected and digitally visible citizens.

- Finally, if this rather extreme worldview actually comes true, GDPs and consumer indices will be measuring very little of the quality of our lives as the role of money becomes a diminished factor in our lived lives.

## UTOPIA OR DYSTOPIA

There have been many books written on the negative impact of digital technologies on work and jobs. Less has been written on how they aid us in our lives, which is often why we acquire them. If some are to be believed, we are on the journey to be replaced by machines that will disempower us and rob us of choice, and many people are ignorant and easily fooled. Some books take a dystopic view of technology – that it is evil. Few books consider the markets and the well-being that have been created because of technology. There is no doubt that digital connectivity creates stress and anxiety for some, and there is a real possibility of alienation for others. While socialising becomes easier, cyberbullying is also an issue. A study of ICT-intensive firms however showed that those who invested both in digital technologies and a range of seven complementary practices gained disproportionately in productivity terms. The predominant thread throughout the study was 'investment in human capital' (Brynjolfsson & Saunders, 2009: ch. 4).

The pace of change has been rapid, and this has created a fissure in much of society. Those who are more engaged become delighted with the latest new digital way to interact with and see the world. The rest are less enthusiastic and still others are dismayed. There is some justification for the dismay, and I attribute this to two main factors.

First, digital connectivity has created mirrors through which we can see ourselves. We have personas through social media such as Twitter or Facebook – these personas are on one hand a reflection of who we are but on the other, not quite who we actually are. That makes both us and others uncomfortable (Mori, 1970). We see ourselves in data collected about us and as sensing creatures; this data creates a tension between our sense perception and our mind perception of ourselves. Mind and material have largely lived separately in our consciousness. We sense ourselves as of this world but when it gets reflected back to us not as sensing but as cognitively perceived data, we think of it as us but not us, and become alarmed when it is held or perceived by others.

Second, the offerings we acquire are increasingly no longer static. When we bought a paperback book back in the day, it remained the same product all through its life. Our computers and smartphones do not remain the same, and because they are not, they are opportunities for firms to collect information about us under the guise of informed consent. We resent having to give out information but are unable to do much about it because we would like to have the product or the service offered. Connected offerings are therefore perceived to be evolving into offerings that coercively take our data. There is a layer of resentment brewing underneath the markets, and it does not take much to evolve these sentiments into inferences of sinister intentions and darker motives of firms.

The push for analytics and big data analysis amplifies a feeling that the firms who hold the data are flaunting their disrespect for the society that coproduced it. The justification for this is that privacy is upheld since the data is anonymised. Yet, the discomfort remains. Anonymity is not an adequate apology for coercing the data out of us in the first place, and many have protested through articles, books and other forms of expression, fuelling the sentiment that we are descending into an Orwellian existence, that we are increasingly under surveillance, fed propaganda and misinformation, and have become a society whose thoughts and words can be manipulated.

It is always fashionable to be a cynic, because being cynical panders to our doubts. The reality is that every phenomenon, event or object that is new is able to afford positive outcomes as well as negative ones. We often like to think of such positives and negatives as forked roads of either/or when in actual fact, it is one road that embodies both.

As the world advances, tensions between positives and negatives have to be recognised and dealt with. Utopian and dystopian visions of the future should both be given a fair hearing. They are part of our quest to take charge of our future rather than fall victim to it. The advancement of cultures and civilisations are precipitated by those who oppose and promote change. A cycle of displacement, negotiation, compromise and displacement again is the process of advancement. Long may these tensions continue.

## CHAPTER 10 REFLECTIONS

Now we have arrived at a point where we can consider markets and the emergent role of 'digital labour', and capture if we can those elusive new economic models. We have also arrived at a point where we can question the simplistic notions of market efficiency – based as they were (or often, still are) on the value-in-exchange. And ownership itself, in a world more attuned to environmental sensitivities, is now beginning to play second fiddle to the values co-created by use.

In this intensely connected networked world of multi-sided markets and their externalities – the knock-on effects – we must now abandon those simple notions. We must reach beyond the basic idea of multipliers – the ripples and impacts of a single action – because without a firm's ability to internalise, to create worth from the co-created values, to capture new revenues, the whole does not become greater than the sum of its parts. However, we see that latent demand from co-created value could create new offerings offered by start-ups and entrepreneurs. Are we seeing the end of the big corporation of many jobs?

We now live in a world of spiralling digital demand, but without commodification we could not translate notions such as 'digital labour' into money and eventually create more economic activity. And commodification is cracking on apace – not least in our personal data, our ultimate asset.

Not everyone is happy, of course, with the digital state we have created for ourselves. Many see this connectivity and openness as creating stress, anxiety, alienation – the road to robotic disempowerment and a loss of choice. Others see differently and not only appreciate new freedoms, new markets, new skills and new opportunities but also acknowledge that this genie cannot be rebottled and put back on the shelf.

There are many reasons for digital discomfort. We may abhor the currently crude or inadequate approximations to ourselves, our personas, as perceived by others. It can be unnerving that the thing we bought is, at the touch of a button, refashioned, updated and repurposed before our very eyes. And assurances of anonymity may do little for our sense of trust or compensate us for trawling through our data drawers with analytical tools that have no respect.

Yet, the positive outcomes as well as the Orwellian negatives must be understood – we cannot elect to choose only one path. We must take charge of the future and not become its victims.

And even if that means going back to the beginning, retracing our steps, reconsidering the way we live and work with others, tackling this tome again and then coming up with some different answers, I hope that you are pleased to have made the journey.

# Postscript

For some time now, I have felt that as a discipline, marketing has become too formulaic and rule-based, not revisiting core concepts in keeping with advances in the markets, especially with the rise of the digital economy. There is a need, at least from my perspective, to return marketing to its roots. Taking Philip Kotler and Kevin Keller's simplest definition, marketing is 'meeting needs, profitably' (Kotler & Keller, 2011). It means the marketing discipline holds both the focus of the customer (in meeting needs) as well as the firm (in being profitable) to an equal regard.

You will have seen this principle play itself out in the book. The book discussed value creation from the perspective of an individual and a customer, considering how our needs are met through products and services, and how that might change with digitisation and connectivity. However, it does not assume these products and services have already been created. Rather, it hopes to inform the design and creation of new and better products and services, which I see as central to the future role of marketing, rather than post hoc rationalisations and selling of offerings already created. You will also see the same discussions addressing the issues faced by the firm, in terms of how it could be commercially viable and profitable in offering these products and services, i.e., its business model.

Marketing has always been twitchy about involving itself as a discipline with engineering and technology (*upstream* marketing, as some would like to call it), but it must. With the speed of how offerings could be (re-)designed and (re-)created, there is a big role for marketing, in representing customers, creating better interfaces and collaborating on requirements and design with engineering and technology, and this cannot be simplistically relegated to just feed-back and focus groups. Dynamic and contextual changes in the use and experience of products and services require better marginal analysis between efficiency and effectiveness considerations of every offering, with value propositions being able to adapt and stay agile while staying viable.

This book proposes a departure from conventional marketing in three major ways.

First, it shifts the focus away from the customer and the psychology (and therefore the notion of profiling) to customers' contexts of value creation – the sociology – and introduces the idea of contextual archetypes. I believe psychology is important but I also believe that social contexts are as well. In other words, the way we behave is just as important as the way we are, and if you speak to many sociologists, they believe both to be one and the same, although the conventional focus of firms have been on who we are rather than what we do. My focus on social contexts does not diminish the psychology of people. Rather, the psychology of individuals is embedded within the social contexts of behaviour, and a focus on contexts enables us to understand better the interactions between them. In the past, data on social contexts would be impossible to obtain. Not today. With digital connectivity and sensor technologies, we are much more able to see and investigate real behaviours and perhaps understand how they relate to our intentions, attitudes and beliefs.

Second, focusing on social contexts would necessarily mean a holistic and systemic approach to lived lives, rather than reducing phenomena to separate domain knowledge and disciplines, as though they remain the same apart as when they come together. I have often quoted Miller and Page (2007) in my papers: 'you cannot understand running water by catching it in a bucket'. Marketing needs to understand its role as part of businesses (its distinctiveness) as well as its role as a part-whole of businesses (its connectiveness).

Finally, this book also proposes a view of marketing as the domain for studying the firm's business model: (1) its value propositions and their viability; (2) its role in the creation of value with its customers; and (3) its ability to capture worth, create markets and earn revenues. All three of these components of a business model, in my view, epitomise the basic principle of 'meeting needs, profitably'. I admit that this is a rather different treatment of marketing, but I have felt for some time now that such a treatment is increasingly necessary.

Such a treatment will necessarily mean that the interfaces between operations and marketing will be increasingly blurred. Traditional exchange value (i.e., worth) has always created tension between choice segmentation and use segmentation and, in turn, interface issues between marketing and operations, since marketing aims to sell by making promises and operations aims to deliver on the promises. For tangible goods, the tension is reduced as operation's task of delivering on sales (passing over the ownership of things) is aligned with marketing's task of selling. For traditional services such as hospitality or healthcare, customers segmented on purchase may not cluster neatly into how they experience the service.

The presence or absence of the customer has major implications for the design of operations, something that researchers in the operations discipline have long discussed. If the future of value is in use in context, be they products or services, both marketing and operations will have to segment based on contexts of use, how outcomes are achieved within the contexts and what revenues can be derived from such systems. This will then have major implications for operations design considerations, and further work is required to identify design rules, which includes the customer (and therefore a role for marketing) in its co-creating activities (Ng et al., 2012). Having more knowledge in this space will spur innovation that will make a real difference in our lives.

Much of the literature on innovation is focused on innovation management of people, process and their organisations, rather than on how to think about making and commercialising a new product or service, which this book focuses on. I differentiate innovation (with roots in management) from what I would term as 'inno-making' (with roots in design, engineering and computing). Both are important but they are quite different. This book focuses on the latter.

Our research continues in this space. In operationalising many of these concepts, we have started on our approach towards moving the research agenda around the IoT.

## THE IoT: AGENDA FOR THE FUTURE

The IoT refers to uniquely identifiable objects (things) and virtual addressability that would create an Internet-like structure for remote locating, sensing, operating and/or actuating of such 'things'. There is a sense that equipping all objects in the world with the ability to be animated and connected could transform lived lives. While the technology to do so is already available, the challenge is calculating how it can be put together and for what purpose. We propose that the IoT should power an information hub acting as a multi-sided market platform for businesses to launch innovative solutions and to serve a market of buyers of such services right at our homes. The platform will then be able to stimulate activity in the economy, leading to new businesses, jobs and wealth creation. It will also help us improve our quality of lives, with the focus of IoT as empowering individuals to live better lives, rather than pushing technology at us.

Many such hubs and their corresponding sensors are starting to find their way into the market. However, services offered through such hubs and sensors make no promises about how they treat our data. Rather, it is assumed that even though the data is that of individuals like us, firms would technically 'own' it even if they may be constrained in using it due to various privacy laws. Without clarity of property rights, markets will have difficulties in forming. Lessons from Facebook and their many altercations with the community around privacy suggest that hubs and other services holding our personal experiential and interactional data will face the same issues. The larger issue is not that of privacy, but of clarity in terms of access rights of personal data so that exchanges can happen, resulting in more services for us, and opportunities for firms.

If you wish to follow our research, please visit www.valueand markets.com and register to be updated on future developments.

# References

Akerlof, G.A. 1970. 'The Market for "Lemons": Quality Uncertainty and the Market Mechanism', *The Quarterly Journal of Economics*, 84(3): 488–500

Arnould, E. 2005. 'Animating the Big Middle', *Journal of Retailing*, 81(2): 89–96

Arnould, E. 2007. 'Consuming Experience. Retrospects and Prospects', in Caru, A. & Cova, B. (eds.), *Consuming Experience*. Routledge, pp. 185–94

Arnould, E.J. & Thompson, C.J. 2005. 'Consumer Culture Theory (CCT): Twenty Years Of Research', *Journal of Consumer Research* 31(March): 868–82

Badinelli, R., Barile, S., Ng, I.C.L., Polese, F., Saviano, M., Di Nauta, P. 2012. 'Viable Service Systems and Decision Making in Service Management', *Journal of Service Management* 23(4): 498–526

Baldwin, C.Y. 2008. 'Where Do Transactions Come From? Modularity, Transactions, and the Boundaries of Firms', *Industrial and Corporate Change* 17(1): 155–95

Barker, C. 2000. *Cultural Studies: Theory And Practice*. Sage Publications

Block, J. 1977. 'Advancing The Psychology Of Personality: Paradigmatic Shift Or Improving The Quality Of Research?' in Magnusson, D. & Endler, N.S. (eds.), *Personality at the Cross-Roads: Current Issues in Interactional Psychology*. Lawrence Erlbaum Associates Inc, pp. 13–21

Bourdieu, P. 1977. *Outline of a Theory of Practice*. Cambridge University Press

Brynjolfsson, E. & Saunders, A. 2009. *Wired for Innovation: How Information Technology is Reshaping the Economy*. MIT Press, ch. 4

Carlo, J.L., Lyytinen, K. and Boland Jr, R.J. 2012. 'Dialectics of Collective Minding: Contradictory Appropriations of Information Technology in a High-Risk Project', *Management Information Systems Quarterly* 36(4): 1081–108.

Chandler, J.D. & Vargo, S.L. 2011. 'Contextualization and Value-In-Context: How Context Frames Exchange', *Marketing Theory*, 11(1): 35–49

Chesbrough, H. 2011. *Open Services Innovation. Rethinking Your Business to Grow and Compete in a New Era*. Jossey-Bass

Christensen, C.M. & Raynor, M.E. 2003. *The Innovator's Solution: Using Good Theory to Solve the Dilemmas of Growth*. Harvard Business School Press

Coase, R.H. 1960. 'The Problem of Social Cost', *Journal of Law and Economics* 3(1): 1–44

Cohen, N.S. 2008. 'The Valorization of Surveillance: Towards a Political Economy of Facebook', *Democratic Communique* 22(1): 5–22

Cova, B. & Dalli, D. 2009. 'Working Consumers: The Next Step in Marketing Theory?', *Marketing Theory* 9: 315–39

Cross, R.C. & Woozley, A.D. 1964. *Plato's Republic: A Philosophical Commentary.* Macmillan

Demirkan, H. & Goul, M. 2006. 'AMCIS 2006 Panel Summary: Towards the Service Oriented Enterprise Vision: Bridging Industry and Academics', *Communications of the Association for Information Systems* 18(1): 26

Demirkan, H., Spohrer, J.C. & Krishna, V. (eds.) 2011. *The Science of Service Systems.* Springer

Dewey, J. 1949. 'The Field of Value' in Lepley, R. (ed.), *Value: A Cooperative Inquiry.* Columbia University Press, p. 66

Eisenmann, T., Parker, G. & Van Alstyne, M.W. 2006. 'Strategies for Two-Sided Markets', *Harvard Business Review* 84(10): 92

Felson, M. & Spaeth, J.L. 1978. 'Community Structure and Collaborative Consumption: A Routine Activity Approach', *American Behavioral Scientist* 21 (March–April): 614–24

Fuchs, C. 2009. 'Class, Knowledge And New Media', *Media, Culture & Society* 32(1): 141–50

Gavetti, G.M., Henderson, R. & Giorgi, S. 2005. *Kodak and The Digital Revolution (A).* Harvard Business School Case, Nov, 705448-PDF-ENG

Gawer, A. & Cusumano, M.A. 2002. *Platform Leadership.* Harvard Business School Press

Gibson, J.J. 1982. 'The Problem of Temporal Order in Stimulation and Perception', in Reed, E. & Jones, R. (eds.), *Reasons for Realism: Selected Essays of James J. Gibson.* Erlbaum, pp. 171–9 (original work published 1966)

Giddens, A. 1984. *The Constitution of Society: Outline of the Theory of Structuration.* University of California Press

Hartman, R.S. 1967. *The Structure of Value.* Southern Illinois Press

Hearn, A. 2008. 'Meat, Mask, Burden: Probing the Contours of the Branded "Self"', *Journal of Consumer Culture* 8(2): 197–217

Heidegger, M. 1996 [1927]. *Being and Time.* State University of New York Press

Henle, P. 1942. 'The Status of Emergence', *Journal of Philosophy* 39: 486–93

Hirshman, E.C. & Holbrook, M.B. 1982. 'Hedonic Consumption: Emerging Concepts, Methods and Propositions', *Journal of Marketing* 46 (Summer): 92–101

Holbrook, M.B. 2006. 'ROSEPEKICECIVEC versus CCV – The Resource-Operant, Skills-Exchanging, Performance-Experiencing, Knowledge-Informed, Competence-Enacting, Coproducer-Involved, Value-Emerging, Customer-Interactive View of Marketing Versus the Concept of Customer Value: 'I Can Get It For You Wholesale', in Lusch, R.L. & Vargo, S.F. (eds.), *The Service-Dominant Logic of Marketing: Dialog, Debate, and Directions*. M.E. Sharpe, pp. 208–23

Husserl, E. 1973 [1939]. *Experience and Judgement*. Churchill, J.S. & Ameriks, K. (trans.). Routledge

Huws, U., Jagger, N. & O'Regan, S. 1999. 'Teleworking and Globalisation', *IES Report* 358: ISBN 1-85184-307-8

IFPI, 2012. *Digital Music Report 2012 – Expanding Choice. Going Global.*

Katz, M.L. & Shapiro, C. 1994. 'Systems Competition and Network Effects', *The Journal of Economic Perspectives* 8(2): 93–115

Kotler, P. & Keller, K. 2011. *Marketing Management*. Prentice Hall

Levin, J. 2013. 'The Economics of Internet Markets', in Acemoglu, D., Arellano, M. & Dekel, E. (eds.), *Advances in Economics and Econometrics*. Cambridge University Press

Levitt, T. 1960. 'Marketing Myopia', *Harvard Business Review*, 38(4): 45–56

Manzerolle, V. 2010. 'Mobilizing the Audience Commodity: Digital Labour in a Wireless World', *Ephemera: Theory of Politics in Organization* 10(4): 455–69

Mattsson, J. 1992. 'A Service Quality Model Based on an Ideal Value Standard', *International Journal of Service Industry Management* 3(3): 18–33

McCracken, G. 1986. 'Culture and Consumption: A Theoretical Account of the Structure and Movement of the Cultural Meaning of Consumer Goods', *Journal of Consumer Research* 13(1): 71–84

Meyera, M.H. & DeToreb, A. 2001. 'PERSPECTIVE: Creating a Platform-Based Approach for Developing New Services', *Journal of Product Innovation Management* 18(3): 188–204

Miller, J.H. & Page, S.E. 2007. *Complex Adaptive Systems: An Introduction to Computational Models of Social Life*. Princeton University Press

Moore, G.E. 1993. *Principia Ethica*. Cambridge University Press

Moorthy, K.S. 1984. 'Market Segmentation, Self-Selection, and Product Line Design', *Marketing Science* 3(4): 288–307

Mori, M. 1970. 'The Uncanny Valley', *Energy* 7(4): 33–5 (in Japanese) www.spectrum.ieee.org/automaton/robotics/humanoids/the-uncanny-valley

Negroponte, N. 1995. *Being Digital*. Vintage

Ng, I.C.L. 2006. 'Differentiation, Self-Selection and Revenue Management', *Journal of Revenue and Pricing Management*, Apr, 5(1):, 2–9

Ng, I.C.L., Williams, J. & Neely, A. 2009a. 'Outcome-Based Contracting: Changing the Boundaries of B2B Customer Relationships: An Executive Briefing', *Advanced Institute of Management (AIM) Research Executive Briefing Series*, October

Ng, I.C.L., Maull, R. & Yip, N. 2009b. 'Outcome-Based Contracts as a Driver For Systems Thinking And Service-Dominant Logic In Service Science: Evidence From The Defence Industry', *European Management Journal* 27(6): 377–87

Ng, I.C.L., Nudurupati, S. & Tasker, P. 2010. 'Value Co-creation in Outcome-based Contracts for Equipment-based Service', *AIM working paper series*, WP No 77 May, www.aimresearch.org/index.php?page=wp-no-77

Ng, I.C.L., Maull, R.S. & Smith, L. 2011. 'Embedding the New Discipline of Service Science' in Demirkan, Spohrer & Krishna (eds.), 1865–4924 pp. 13–35

Ng, I.C.L. & Briscoe, G. 2012. 'Value, Variety and Viability: New Business Models for Co-Creation in Outcome-based Contracts', *International Journal of Service Science, Management, Engineering, and Technology* 3(3): 26–48

Ng, I.C.L., Guo, L. & Ding, Y. 2012. 'Continuing Use of Information Technology as Value Co-creation: The Role of Contextual Variety and Means Drivenness', *WMG Service Systems Research Group Working Paper Series*, paper number 07/12, ISSN 2049–4297. http://bit.ly/yYzJ9X

Ng, I.C.L., Parry, G., Maull, R., Smith, L., Briscoe, G. 2012. 'Transitioning from a Goods-Dominant to a Service-Dominant Logic: Visualising the Value Proposition of Rolls Rolls-Royce', *Journal of Service Management* 23(3): 416–39

Ng, I.C.L., Ponsignon, F., Maull, R.S. & Vargo, S.L. 2012. *The Shifting Boundaries of Marketing and Operations under Service Dominant Logic*. 2012 INFORMS Manufacturing and Service Operations Management (MSOM), Columbia University, June 17–19

Ng, I.C.L. & Smith, L.A. 2012. 'An Integrative Framework of Value', *Review of Marketing Research Special issue on Toward a Better Understanding of the Role of Value in Markets and Marketing*, Vargo, S.L. & Lusch, R.F. (eds.) 9, pp. 207–43

Ng, I.C.L., Ding, X. & Yip, N.K.T. 2013. 'Outcome-based Contracts as New Business Model: The Role of Partnership and Value-driven Relational Assets', *Industrial Marketing Management*, in press, available at http://dx.doi.org/10.1016/j.indmarman.2013.05.009

Normann, R. 2001. *Reframing Business: When the Map Changes the Landscape*. John Wiley & Sons Inc

Normann, R. & Ramírez, R. 1994. *Designing Interactive Strategy: From Value Chain to Value Constellation*. John Wiley & Sons

Orlikowski, W.J. 2007. 'Sociomaterial Practices: Exploring Technology at Work', *Organization Studies* 28, 1435–48

Orlikowski, W.J. 2009. 'The Sociomateriality of Organizational Life: Considering Technology in Management Research', *Cambridge Journal of Economics* 34: 125–41

Osterwalder, A. & Pigneur, Y. 2010. *Business Model Generation: A Handbook for Visionaries, Game Changers, and Challengers*. Wiley and Sons

Osterwalder, A., Pigneur, Y. & Tucci, C.L. 2005. 'Clarifying Business Models: Origins, Present, and Future of the Concept', *Communications of the Association for Information Systems* 16(1): 1–25

Payne, A. & Frow, P. 2005. 'A Strategic Framework for Customer Relationship Management', *Journal of Marketing* 69(4): 167–76

Payne, A., Storbacka, K. & Frow, P. 2008. 'Managing the Co-Creation of Value', *Academy of Marketing Science* 36(1): 83–96

Penzias, A. 1995. *Harmony: Business, Technology and Life After Paperwork*. HarperBusiness

Pickering, J. 2007. 'Affordances are Signs', *Cognition, Communication, Co-operation* 5(2) ISSN 1726–670X. http://tripleC.uti.at.

Pissarides, C. 1985. 'Short-run Equilibrium Dynamics of Unemployment, Vacancies, and Real Wages', *American Economic Review* 75: 676–90

Porter, M. 2004. *Competitive Advantage*. Free Press

Prahalad, C.K. & Ramaswamy, V. 2000. 'Co-opting Customer Competence', *Harvard Business Review* 78 (January), 79–90

Reckwitz, A. 2002. 'Toward a Theory of Social Practices: A Development in Culturalist Theorizing', *European Journal of Social Theory* 5(2): 243–63

Rochet, J.-C. & Tirole, J. 2003. 'Platform Competition in Two-Sided Markets', *Journal of the European Economic Association* 1: 990–1029

Rogers, E.M. 1962. *Diffusion of Innovations*. Free Press

Rothschild, M. & Stiglitz, J. 1976. 'Equilibrium in Competitive Insurance Markets: An Essay on the Economics of Imperfect Information', *The Quarterly Journal of Economics* 90(4): 629–49

Sandel, M.J. 2000. 'What Money Can't Buy: The Moral Limits of Markets', *Tanner Lectures on Human Values* 21: 87–122

Sarasvathy, S.D. 2001. 'Causation and Effectuation: Toward a Theoretical Shift from Economic Inevitability to Entrepreneurial Contingency', *The Academy of Management Review* 26(2): 243–63

Saren, M., Maclaran, P., Goulding, C., Elliott, R., Shankar, A. & Catterall, M. (eds.) 2007. *Critical Marketing: Defining The Field*. Butterworth-Heinemann

Say, J. 1821. *A Treatise On The Political Economy*. Wells and Lilly

Schatzki, T.R. 1996. *Social Practices: A Wittgensteinian Approach to Human Activity and the Social*. Cambridge University Press

Schroeder, J.E. 2007. *Critical Marketing: Insights for Informed Research and Teaching*. Butterworth-Heinemann

Shankar, A., Cherrier, H. & Canniford, R. 2006. 'Consumer Empowerment: A Foucauldian Interpretation', *European Journal of Marketing* 40(9/10): 1013–30

Shapiro, C. & Varian, H.R. 1999. *Information Rules: A Strategic Guide to the Network Economy*. Harvard Business Press

Shirky, C. 2010. *Cognitive Surplus: Creativity and Generosity in a Connected Age*. Penguin

Simon, H.A. 1991. 'Bounded Rationality and Organizational Learning', *Organization Science* 2(1): 125–34

Simon, H.A. 1996. *The Sciences of the Artificial*. MIT Press

Smith, A. 1904 [1776]. *An Inquiry Into The Nature And Causes Of The Wealth Of Nations*. W. Strahan and T. Cadell

Smythe, D.W. 1981. *Dependency Road: Communications, Capitalism, Consciousness and Canada*. Ablex

Spohrer, J., Maglio, P.P., Bailey, J. & Gruhl, D. 2007. 'Steps Toward a Science of Service Systems', *Computer* 40(1)(January): 71–7

Sraffa, P. 1960. *Production of Commodities by Means of Commodities: Prelude to a Critique of Economic Theory*. Vora and Co. Publishers PVT Ltd

Strang, D. & Meyer, J.W. 1993. 'Institutional Conditions for Diffusion', *Theory and Society* 22(4): 487–511

Tapscott, D. 1997. *The Digital Economy: Promise, and Peril in the Age of Networked Intelligence*. McGraw-Hill

Teece, D.J. 2010. 'Business Models, Business Strategy and Innovation', *Long Range Planning* 43(2–3): 172–94

Toffler, A. 1984. *Future Shock*. Bantam

Turkle, S. 2011. *Alone Together: Why We Expect More from Technology and Less from Each Other*. Basic Books

Vargo, S.L. & Lusch, R.F. 2004. 'Evolving to a New Dominant Logic For Marketing', *Journal of Marketing* 68: 1–17

Vargo, S.L. & Lusch, R.F. 2008. 'Service-Dominant Logic: Continuing the Evolution', *Journal of the Academy of Marketing Science* 36(1): 1–10

Vargo, S.L. & Morgan, F.W. 2005. 'Services in Society and Academic Thought: A Historical Analysis', *Journal of Macromarketing* 25(1): 42–53

Vargo, S.L., Maglio, P.P. & Akaka, M.A. 2008. 'On Value and Value Co-Creation: A Service Systems and Service Logic Perspective', *European Management Journal* 26: 145–52

Vargo, S.L. & Lusch, R.F. 2011. 'It's all B2B ... and Beyond: Toward a Systems Perspective of the Market', *Industrial Marketing Management* 40(2): 181–7

Venkatesh, R. & Mahajan, V. 1993. 'A Probabilistic Approach to Pricing a Bundle of Products or Services', *Journal of Marketing Research* 30(Nov): 494–508

Warde, A. 2005. 'Consumption and Theories of Practices', *Journal of Consumer Culture* 5(2):131–53

Wessel, M. & Christensen, C.M. 2012. 'Surviving Disruption', *Harvard Business Review* 90(12): 56–64,

Wilson, R. 1993. *Nonlinear Pricing*. Oxford University Press

Yoo, Y.J., Boland, R.J., Lyytinen, K. & Majchrzak, A. 2012. 'Organizing for Innovation in the Digitized World', *Organisation Science* 23(5), Sep-Oct: 1398–408

# Index